Pretty Stitches

Jayne Schofield

Tuva Publishing

www.tuvapublishing.com

Address Merkez Mah. Cavusbasi Cad. No:71
Cekmekoy - Istanbul 34782 / Turkey
Tel: +9 0216 642 62 62

Pretty Stitches

First Print 2016 / December

All Global Copyrights Belong To
Tuva Tekstil ve Yayıncılık Ltd.

Content Cross Stitch

Editor in Chief Ayhan DEMİRPEHLİVAN
Project Editor Kader DEMİRPEHLİVAN
Designer Jayne SCHOFIELD
Technical Editors Leyla ARAS, Büşra ESER
Graphic Designers Ömer ALP, Abdullah BAYRAKÇI
Assistant Zilal ÖNEL
Photograph Tuva Publishing

ISBN: 978-605-9192-23-1

Printing House
Bilnet Matbaacılık ve Ambalaj San. A.Ş.

 TuvaYayincilik TuvaPublishing
 TuvaYayincilik TuvaPublishing

Introduction

I am delighted to present this book to you, full of beautiful cross stitch projects designed by myself.

Within its pages is a collection of stitching patterns bursting with prettiness. The themes that I have included reflect an array of things that I love, including family, summer gardens, butterflies, cup cakes, baby samplers and wedding celebrations.

I have drawn on my own surroundings as inspiration for this book, taking snapshots from my garden to work from and including designs based around my love of vintage porcelain.

Many of the samplers within can be personalised by using one of the alphabets provided in this book and given as presents for family or friends.

All the patterns were designed to bring many happy hours of stitching and I hope that you enjoy working through its pages.

Jayne

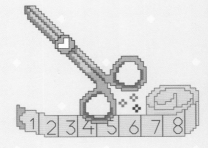

Contents

Summer Birdhouse

The inspiration for this design came from my own garden. We have a small birdhouse high up in one of the fruit trees and this is frequently visited by an arrayof beautiful garden birds.

This design has many interesting areas to stitch. With its colourful blooms and two chirping songbirds, this pretty design would be ideal framed or perhaps made into a cushion for the garden room.

Fabric DMC 16 ct Aida DM844/Blanc
Fabric Size 40 x 42 cm
Pattern Size 18 x 21 cm
Thread DMC Stranded Cotton

Cross Stitch 2 strands
Backstitch 1 strand

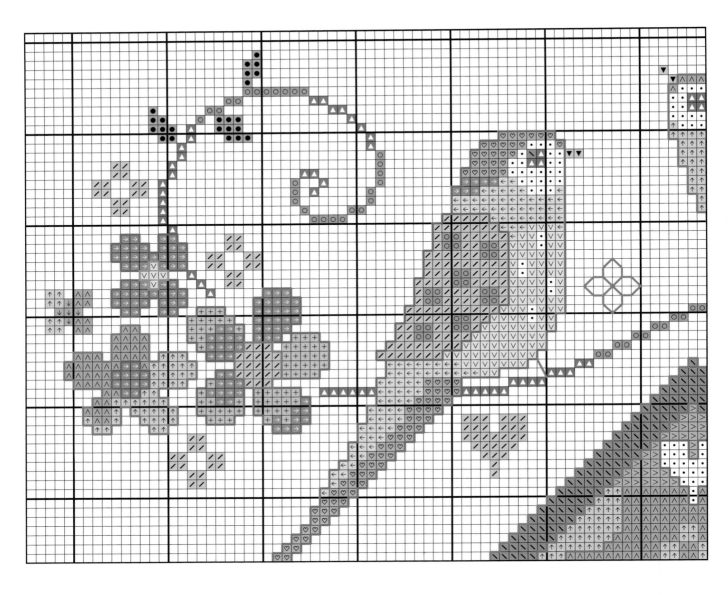

Mouline
Stranded Cotton Art. 117

∴	B5200	↓↓	3819	✹✹	3810	○○	209	← ←	818	╱ B5200	╱ 3804
∨∨	727	●●	564	▲▲	3746	>>	3609	♥♥	957	╱ 3810	╱ 970
▼▼	725	↑↑	747	◥◥	340	++	605	➡➡	603	╱ 3819	
<<	165	∧∧	964	╱╱	211	××	3689	✢✢	970	╱ 3746	

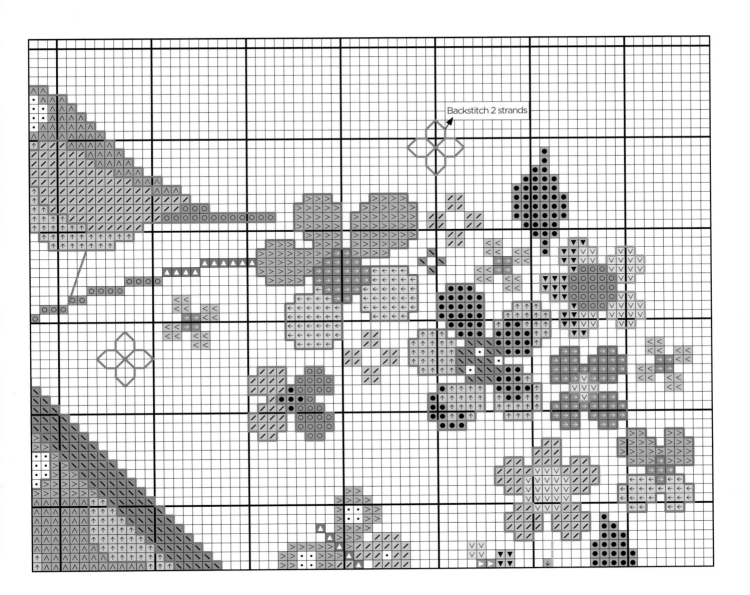

Backstitch 2 strands

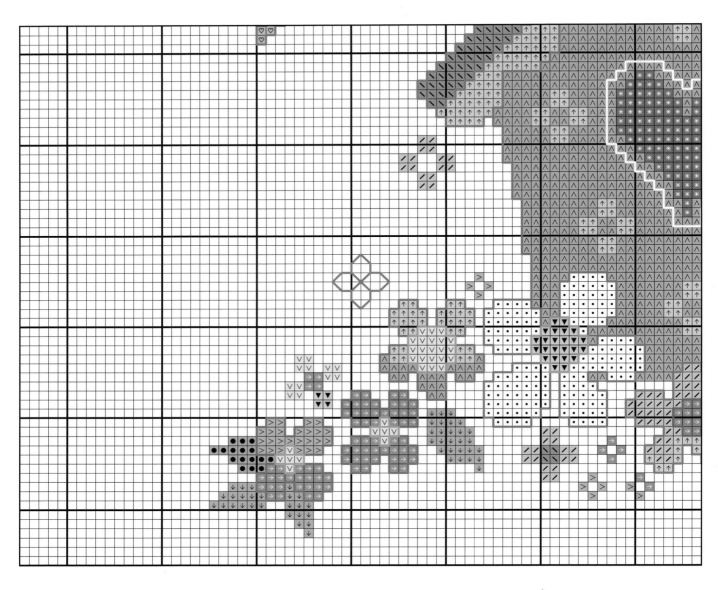

Mouliné
Stranded Cotton Art. 117

Symbol	Color	Symbol	Color	Symbol	Color	Symbol	Color	Symbol	Color	Symbol	Color	Symbol	Color
∴	B5200	↓↓	3819	✱✱	3810	○○	209	←←	818	/	B5200	/	3804
∨∨	727	●●	564	▲▲	3746	>>	3609	♡♡	957	/	3810	/	970
▼▼	725	↑↑	747	＼＼	340	++	605	→→	603	/	3819		
<<	165	∧∧	964	⁄⁄	211	××	3689	⋈	970	/	3746		

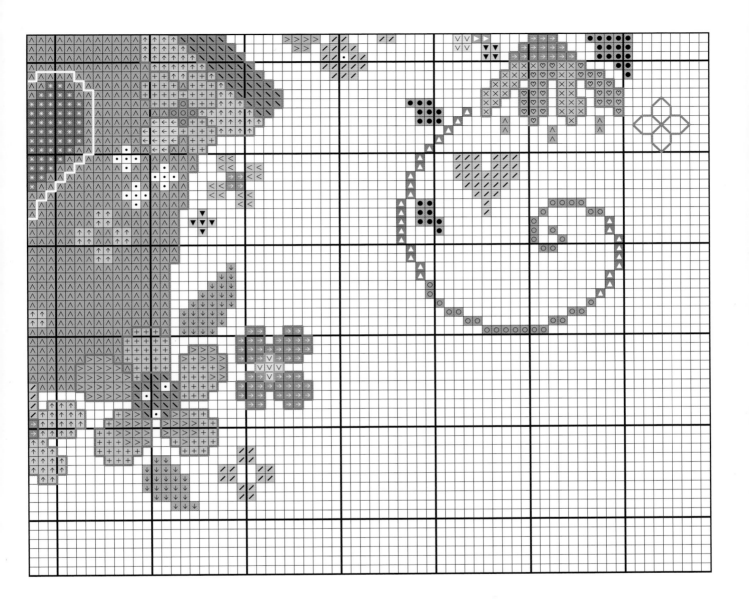

Floral Birdcage

This bright and colourful design is bursting with, butterflies and richly coloured delicate blooms. The pretty birdcage is similar to the one I have in my sitting room and the inspiration for the flower shapes came from my own garden.

This design would make a lovely gift for a wedding couple and could be easily personalised using one of the alphabets included in this book. The masses of detail within this design make it interesting and a joy to stitch.

Fabric DMC 16 ct Aida DM844/Blanc
Fabric Size 40 x 48 cm
Pattern Size 17 x 26 cm
Thread DMC Stranded Cotton

Cross Stitch 2 strands
Backstitch 1 strand

Backstitch 2 strands

Backstitch 2 strands

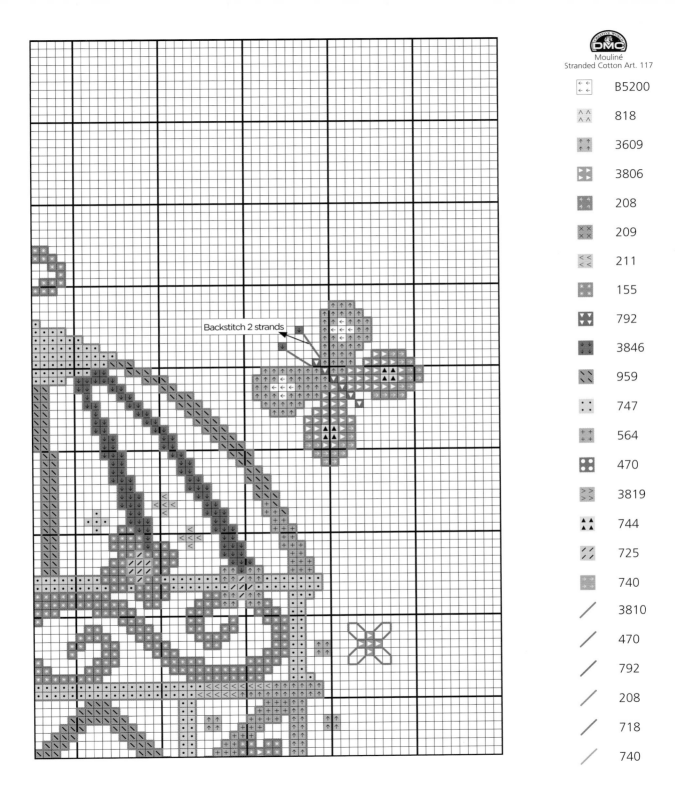

Backstitch 2 strands

Symbol	DMC
← ← ← ←	B5200
∧ ∧ ∧ ∧	818
↑ ↑ ↑ ↑	3609
▶ ▶ ▶ ▶	3806
4 4 4 4	208
× × × ×	209
< < < <	211
✳ ✳ ✳ ✳	155
▼ ▼ ▼ ▼	792
▪ ▪ ▪ ▪	3846
＼ ＼ ＼ ＼	959
∶ ∶	747
+ + + +	564
● ● ● ●	470
> > > >	3819
▲ ▲ ▲ ▲	744
／ ／ ／ ／	725
→ → → →	740
／	3810
／	470
／	792
／	208
／	718
／	740

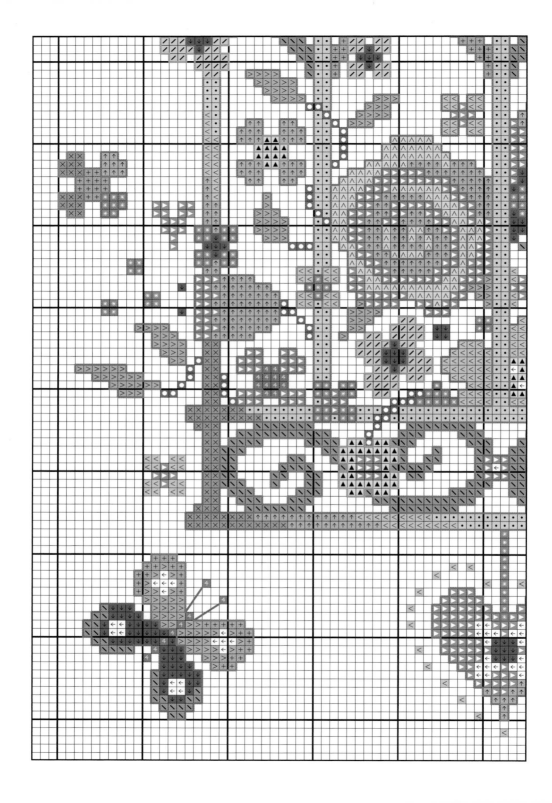

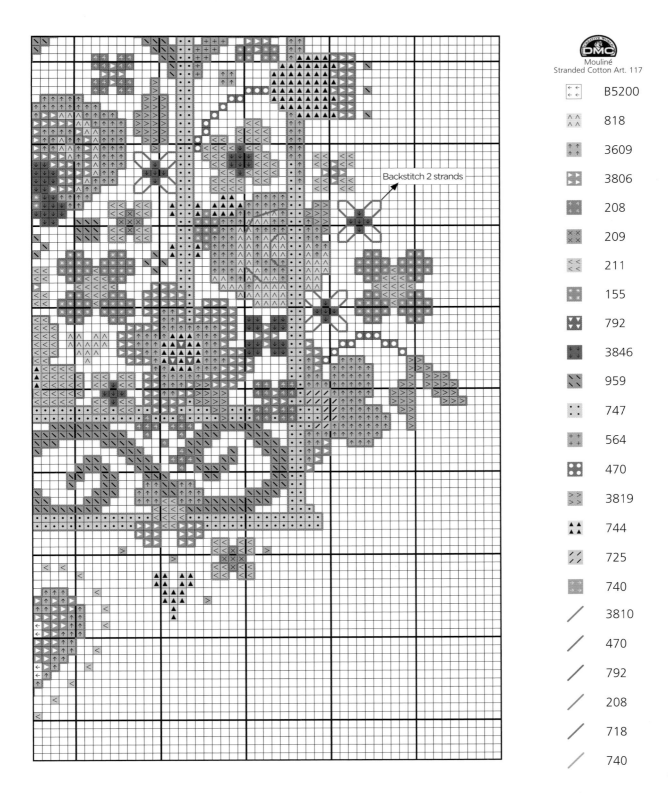

Backstitch 2 strands

DMC
Mouliné
Stranded Cotton Art. 117

Symbol	Code
← ← / ← ←	B5200
^ ^ / ^ ^	818
↑ ↑ / ↑ ↑	3609
▶ ▶ / ▶ ▶	3806
4 4 / 4 4	208
✕ ✕ / ✕ ✕	209
< < / < <	211
✳ ✳ / ✳ ✳	155
▼▼ / ▼▼	792
↓ ↓ / ↓ ↓	3846
＼＼ / ＼＼	959
∶ ∶ / ∶ ∶	747
+ + / + +	564
● ● / ● ●	470
> > / > >	3819
▲ ▲ / ▲ ▲	744
╱╱ / ╱╱	725
→ → / → →	740
╱	3810
╱	470
╱	792
╱	208
╱	718
╱	740

17

Floral Home Sampler

Bring a bit of your summer garden into your home with this richly adorned Floral Home Sampler. It is a celebration of garden delights. Dancing butterflies and spotted ladybirds nestle within the pretty flowers and sweet hearts. The inspiration for this design came from a patch of wild flowers I came across while walking near my home.

There are lots of interesting elements to stitch in this design and the finished piece would make an ideal cushion or framed and hung on a sunny wall..

Fabric DMC 16 Aida DM844/Blanc
Fabric Size 42 x 42 cm
Pattern Size 20,5 x 20,5 cm
Thread DMC Stranded Cotton

Cross Stitch 2 strands
Backstitch 1 strand

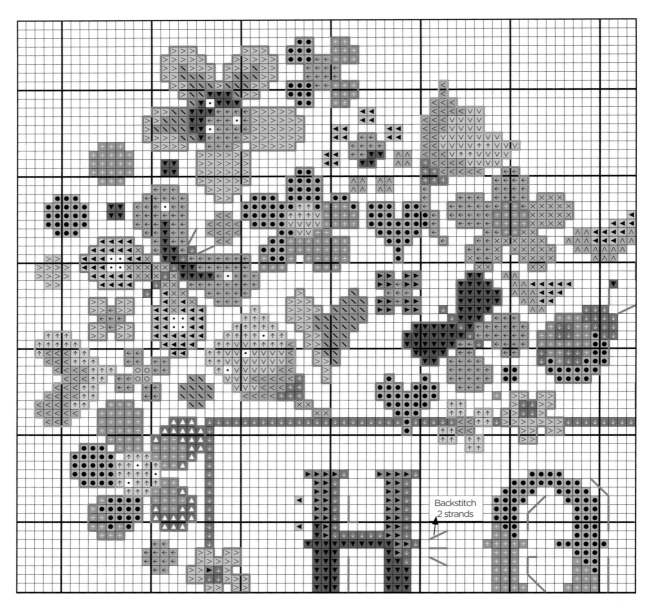

Mouliné
Stranded Cotton Art. 117

Symbol	Color	Symbol	Color	Symbol	Color	Symbol	Color	Symbol	Color	Symbol	Color	Symbol	Color
⠒⠒	B5200	∧∧	3819	▼▼	3846	>>	211	<<	3854	/	3807	/	740
↑↑	726	××	955	✤	3807	∷	3609	✤	740	/	3849	/	3805
∨∨	725	✦	912	▶▶	340	✤	3806	▷▷	3713	/	906		
◀◀	165	←	964	＼＼	209	▲▲	3805						

Backstitch
2 strands

20

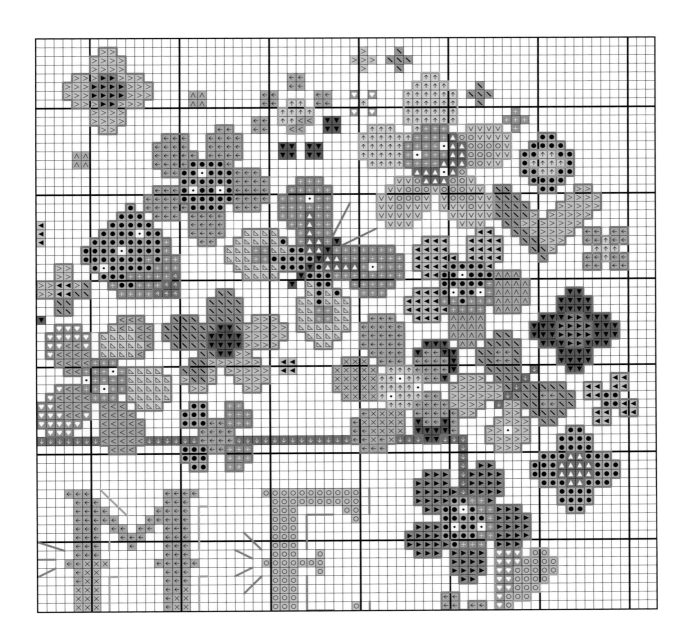

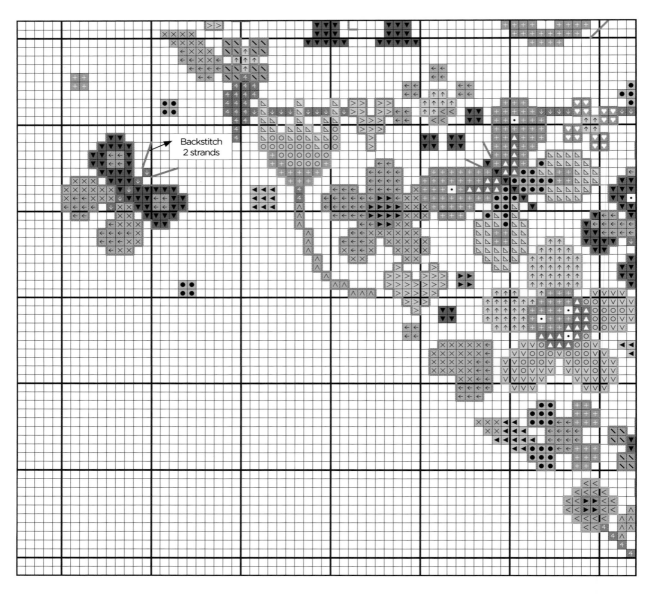

Backstitch
2 strands

∴	B5200	∧∧	3819	▼▼	3846	⌐⌐	211	<<	3854	/	3807	/	740
↑↑	726	××	955	↓↓	3807	••	3609	▼▼	740	/	3849	/	3805
∨∨	725	⁴⁴	912	▶▶	340	++	3806	△△	3713	/	906		
◀◀	165	←←	964	╲╲	209	▲▲	3805						

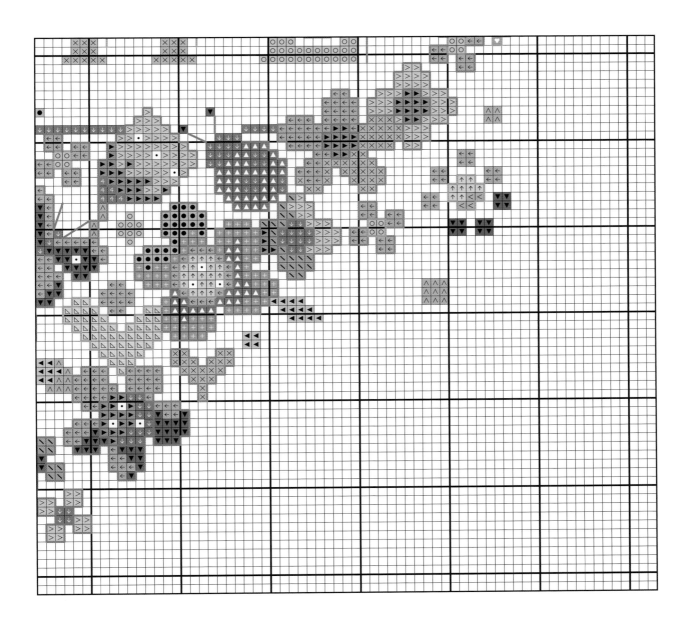

24

Summer Days

This pretty lace trimmed handbag is evocative of those summer days, getting dressed up for afternoon tea or to attend a garden party. With its pretty blue bow and matching bunting this design is very feminine and would make an ideal gift for a special lady.

Fabric DMC 16 ct Aida DM844/Blanc
Fabric Size 42 x 45 cm
Pattern Size 19,5 x 21,5 cm
Thread DMC Stranded Cotton

Cross Stitch 2 strands
Backstitch 1 strand

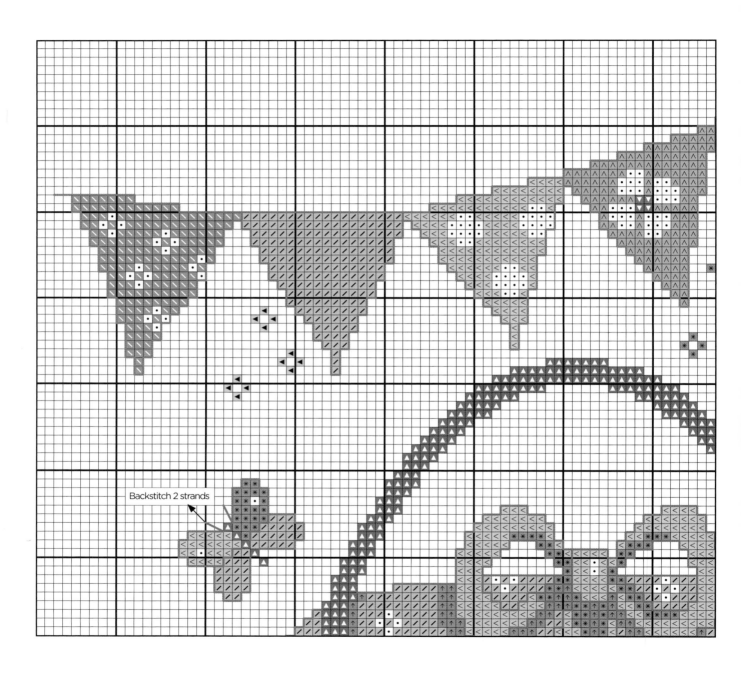

Backstitch 2 strands

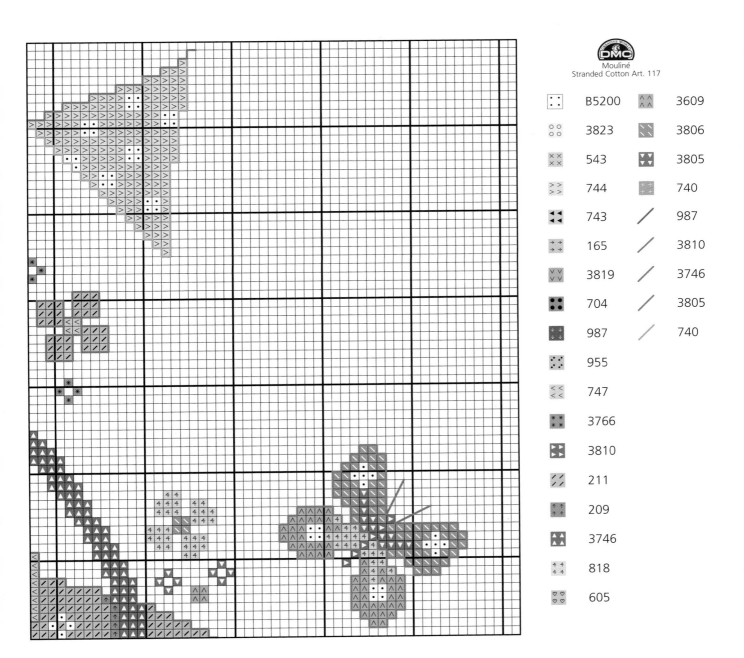

Mouliné
Stranded Cotton Art. 117

⠒	B5200	^ ^	3609
○ ○	3823	＼＼	3806
× ×	543	▼▼	3805
＞＞	744	▦	740
◀◀	743	╱	987
→→	165	╱	3810
∨∨	3819	╱	3746
●●	704	╱	3805
↓↓	987	╱	740
⠂	955		
＜＜	747		
✱✱	3766		
◤◥	3810		
╱╱	211		
↑↑	209		
▲▲	3746		
4 4	818		
♡♡	605		

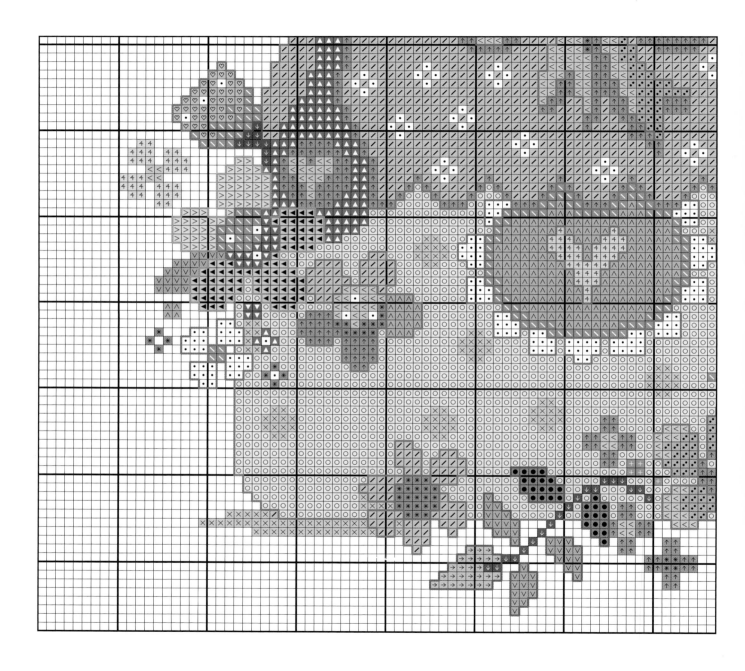

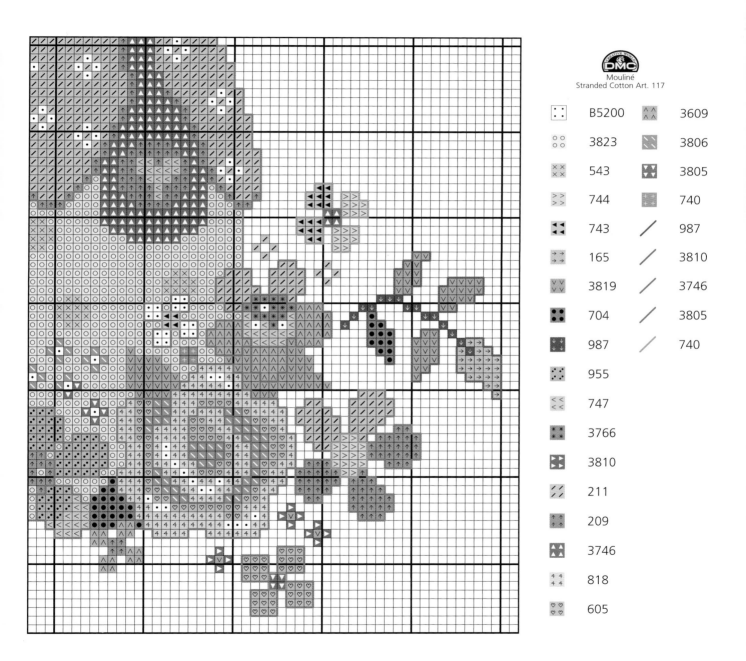

DMC
Mouliné
Stranded Cotton Art. 117

::	B5200	^^ ^^	3609
°°	3823	◥◥	3806
×× ××	543	▼▼	3805
>> >>	744	╪	740
◀◀	743	╱	987
→→ →→	165	╱	3810
∨∨	3819	╱	3746
●● ●●	704	╱	3805
▼▼	987	╱	740
∴∴	955		
<< <<	747		
✳✳	3766		
▶▶	3810		
╱╱	211		
↑↑	209		
▲▲	3746		
4 4 4 4	818		
♡♡	605		

Butterfly Garden

I am lucky enough to be able to look out over my garden while I work. I have a pink rose tree that borders one of my flower beds and this patch is frequently visited by an array of different coloured butterflies. It is here that I took my inspiration for this design. I have included lots of different areas of interest which makes it a joy to stitch and there are elements that can be stitched on their own to form other designs.

The butterflies would be ideal as greeting cards or stitched onto the corner of a pillow case. A row of single flowers could be used to border a tablecloth or runner.

Fabric DMC 16 ct Aida DM844/Blanc
Fabric Size 45 x 45 cm
Pattern Size 23 x 23 cm
Thread DMC Stranded Cotton

Cross Stitch 2 strands
Backstitch 1 strand

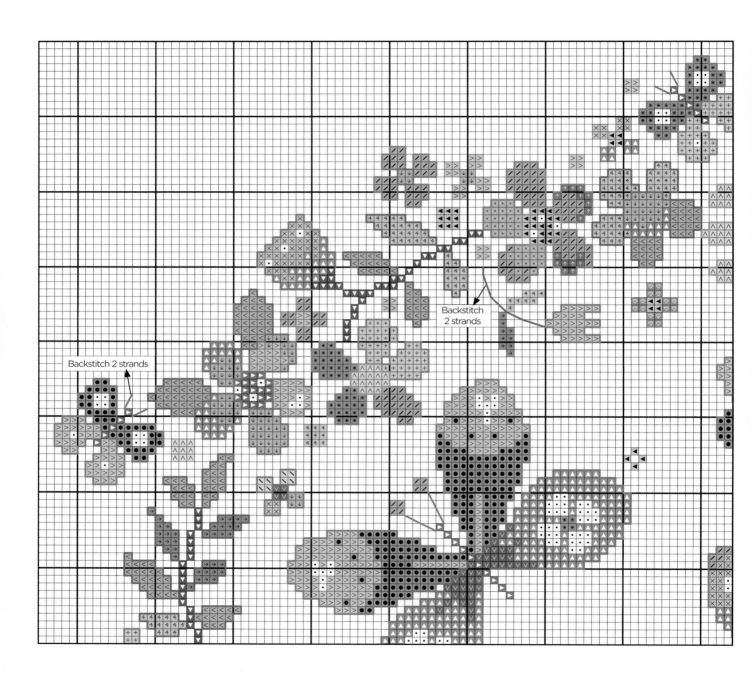

Backstitch 2 strands

Backstitch
2 strands

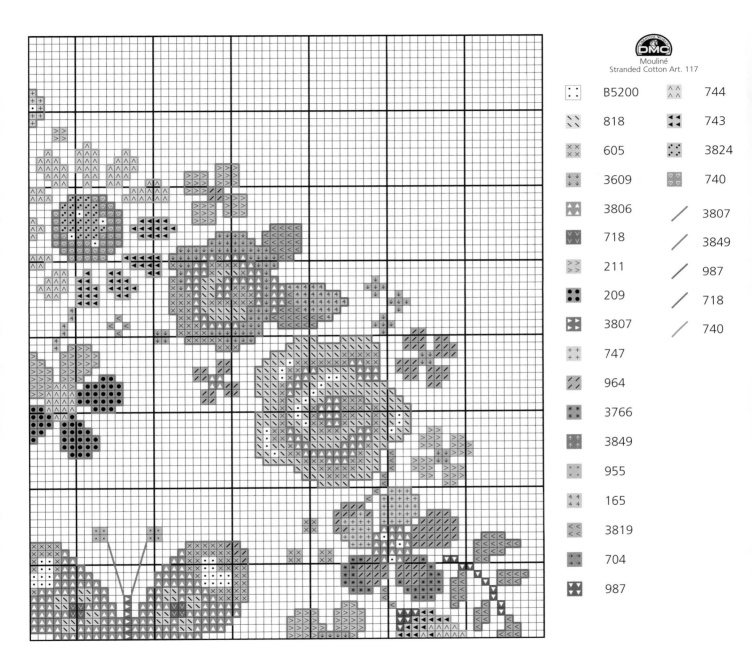

DMC
Mouliné
Stranded Cotton Art. 117

B5200			744	
818			743	
605			3824	
3609			740	
3806		/	3807	
718		/	3849	
211		/	987	
209		/	718	
3807		/	740	
747				
964				
3766				
3849				
955				
165				
3819				
704				
987				

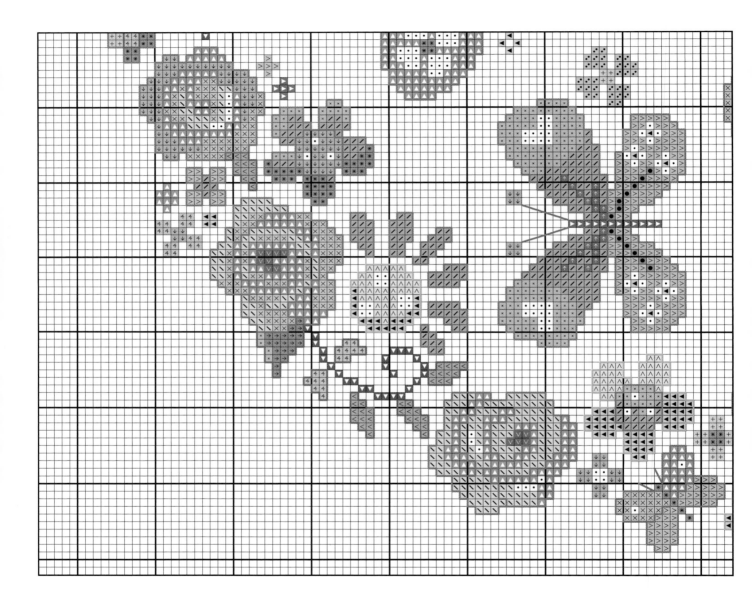

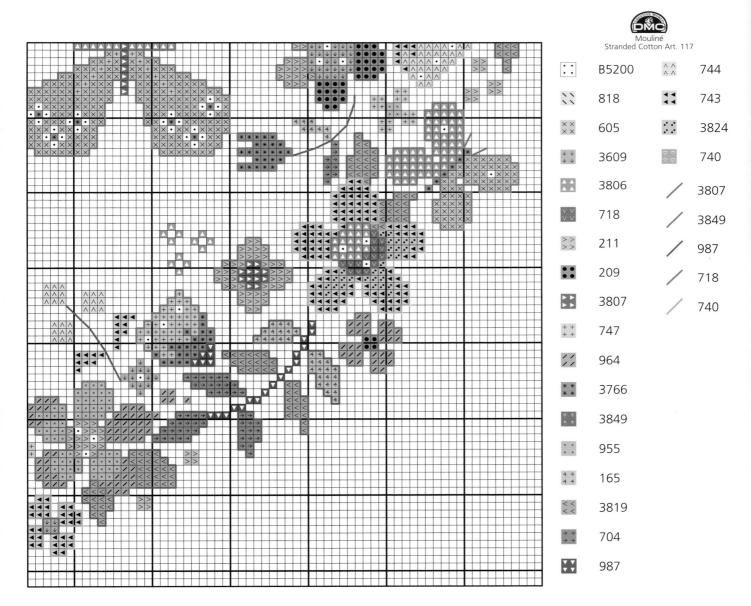

DMC
Mouliné
Stranded Cotton Art. 117

∴ B5200	∧∧ 744
⟍⟍ 818	◄◄ 743
✕✕ 605	∴ 3824
↓↓ 3609	740
▲▲ 3806	╱ 3807
∨∨ 718	╱ 3849
>> 211	╱ 987
●● 209	╱ 718
►► 3807	╱ 740
++ 747	
∕∕ 964	
✳✳ 3766	
↑↑ 3849	
✕✕ 955	
44 165	
<< 3819	
→→ 704	
▼▼ 987	

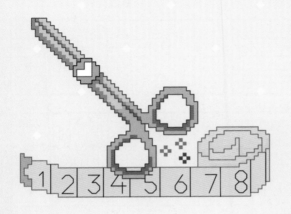

Craft Sampler

This Craft Sampler is inspired by my passion for sewing and includes a selection of items taken from my sewing box. Real buttons could be used in place of the stitched versions to add extra interest to your finished stitched piece.

The finished stitched design would make an ideal cover for a stitching journal or framed and hung in a sewing room. Each element could be stitched as a single design and used to adorn a button box, bobbin tin or needle case.

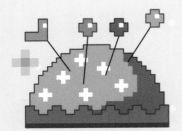

Fabric DMC 16 ct Aida DM844/Blanc
Fabric Size 40 x 45 cm
Pattern Size 17,5 x 22,5 cm
Thread DMC Stranded Cotton

Cross Stitch 2 strands
Backstitch 1 strand

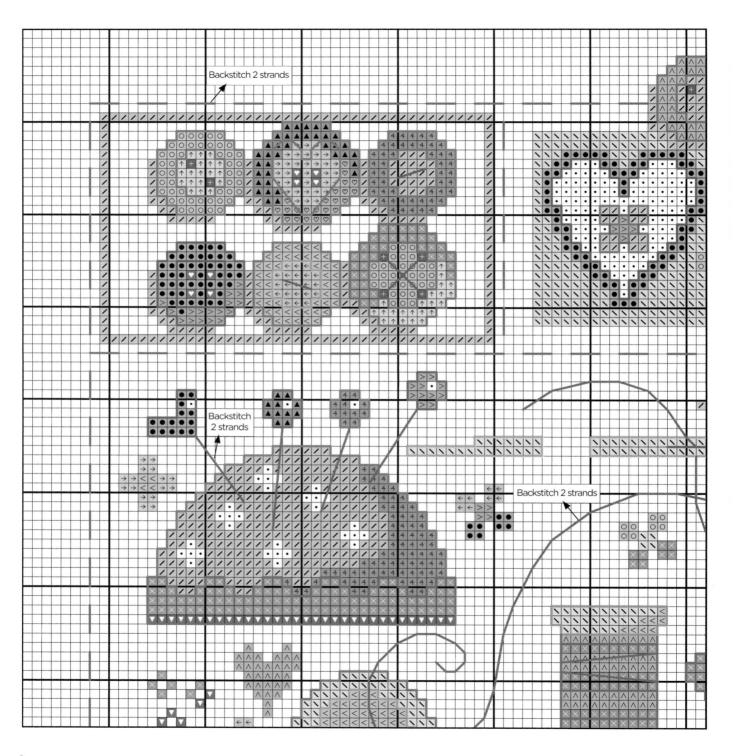

Backstitch 2 strands

Backstitch 2 strands

Backstitch 2 strands

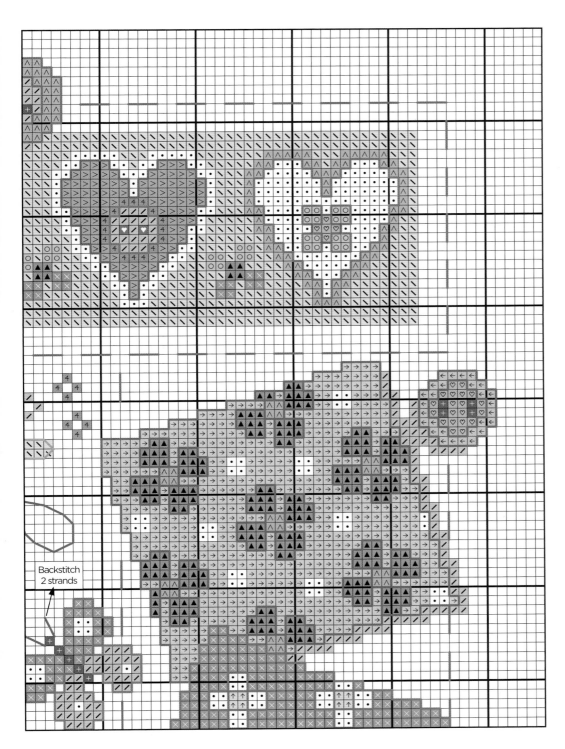

DMC
Mouliné
Stranded Cotton Art. 117

::	B5200	/	987
vv	Ecru	/	3848
↑↑	818	/	792
°°	605	/	3746
XX	3806	/	718
∧∧	3609	/	740
▼▼	718	/	3778
//	211		
44	209		
♥♥	3746		
++	792		
→→	747		
>>	964		
▲▲	3766		
♡♡	955		
••	3819		
←←	165		
\\	744		
<<	3824		

Backstitch
2 strands

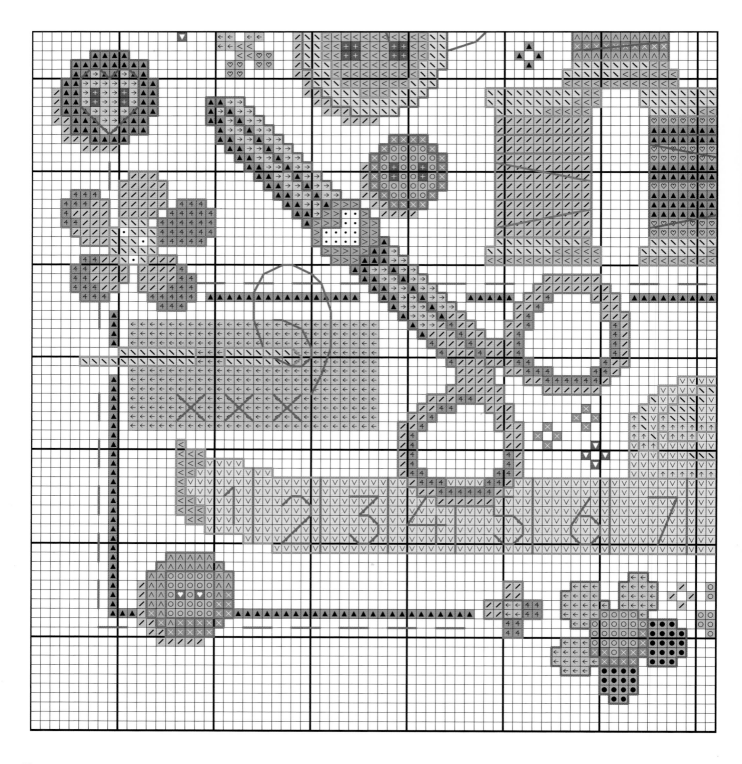

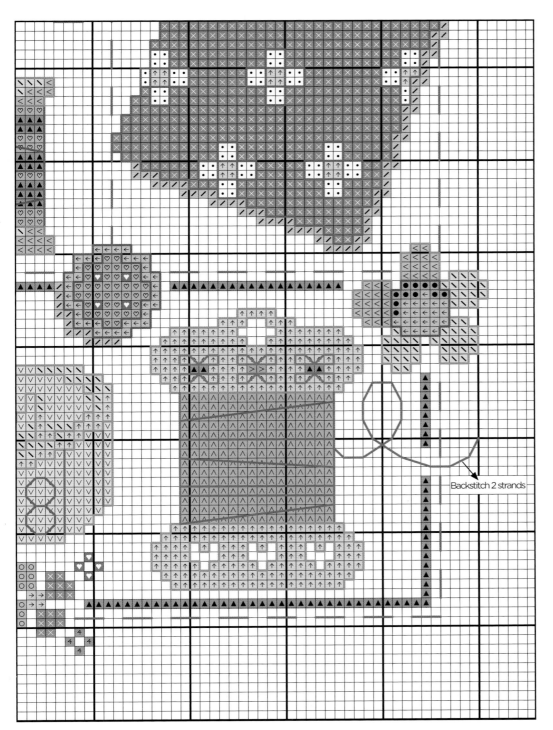

Mouliné
Stranded Cotton Art. 117

∷	B5200	╱	987		
∨∨	Ecru	╱	3848		
↑↑	818	╱	792		
○○	605	╱	3746		
××	3806	╱	718		
∧∧	3609	╱	740		
▼▼	718	╱	3778		
╱╱	211				
44	209				
♥♥	3746				
✚✚	792				
→→	747				
>>	964				
▲▲	3766				
♡♡	955				
●●	3819				
←←	165				
╲╲	744				
<<	3824				

Backstitch 2 strands

41

Floral Tea Cups

I like to collect pretty vintage china tea cups. I love all the different shapes and delicate patterns that adorn them. This is where the inspiration came from for this design.

This imagery is evocative of tea in the garden, surrounded by colourful flowerbeds on long summer days. This stitched piece would be ideal framed and hung in a pretty kitchen or dining room, or bordered with soft pink fabric and made into a cushion to sit in a garden room.

Fabric DMC 28 ct Linen DM432/B5200
Fabric Size 45 x 45 cm
Pattern Size 22,5 x 23,5 cm
Thread DMC Stranded Cotton

Cross Stitch 2 strands
Backstitch 1 strand

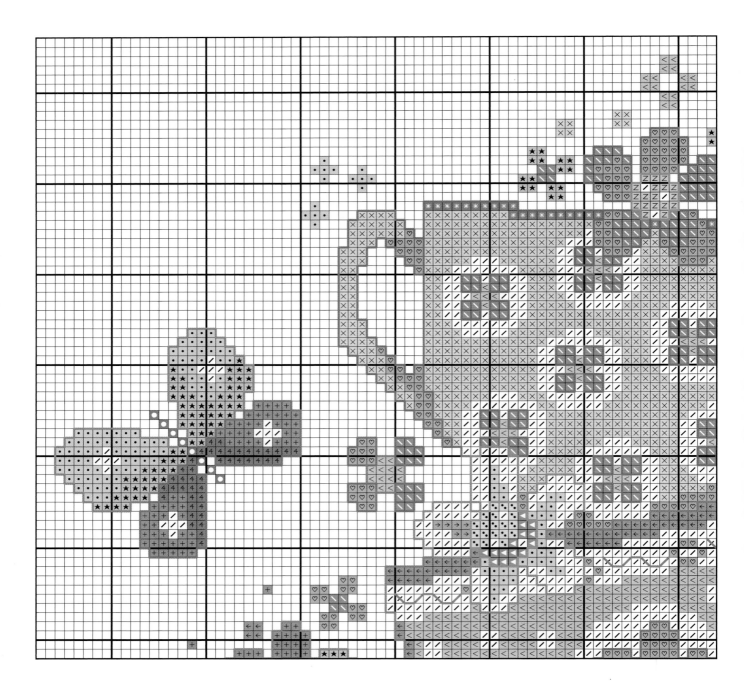

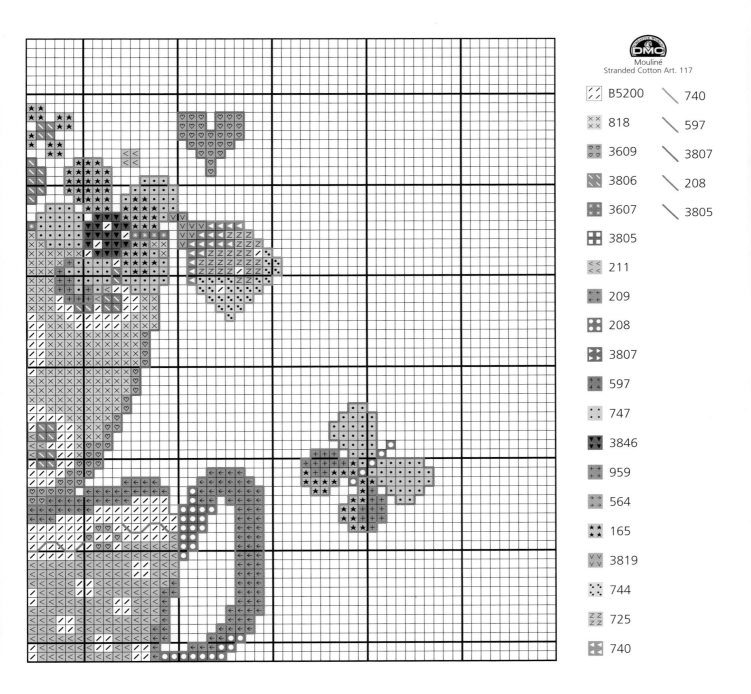

DMC
Mouliné
Stranded Cotton Art. 117

B5200		740	
818		597	
3609		3807	
3806		208	
3607		3805	
3805			
211			
209			
208			
3807			
597			
747			
3846			
959			
564			
165			
3819			
744			
725			
740			

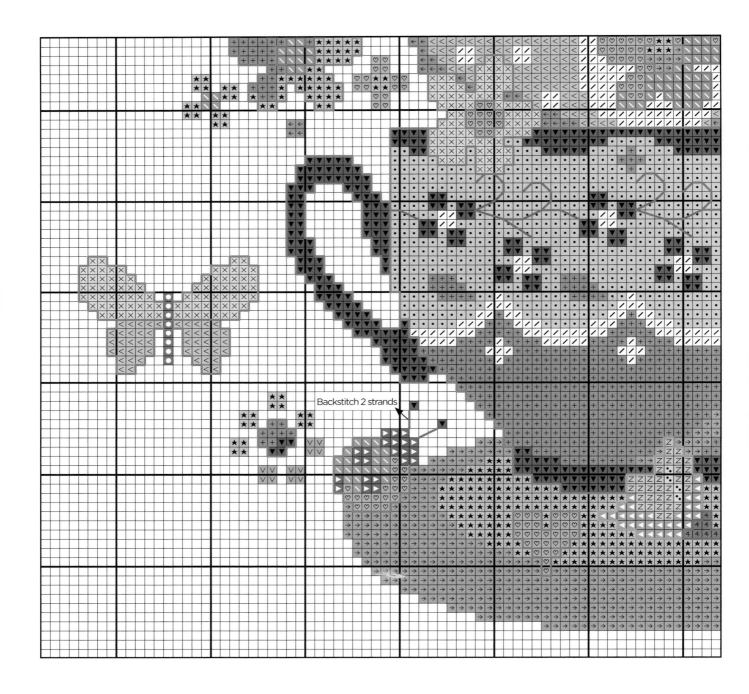

Backstitch 2 strands

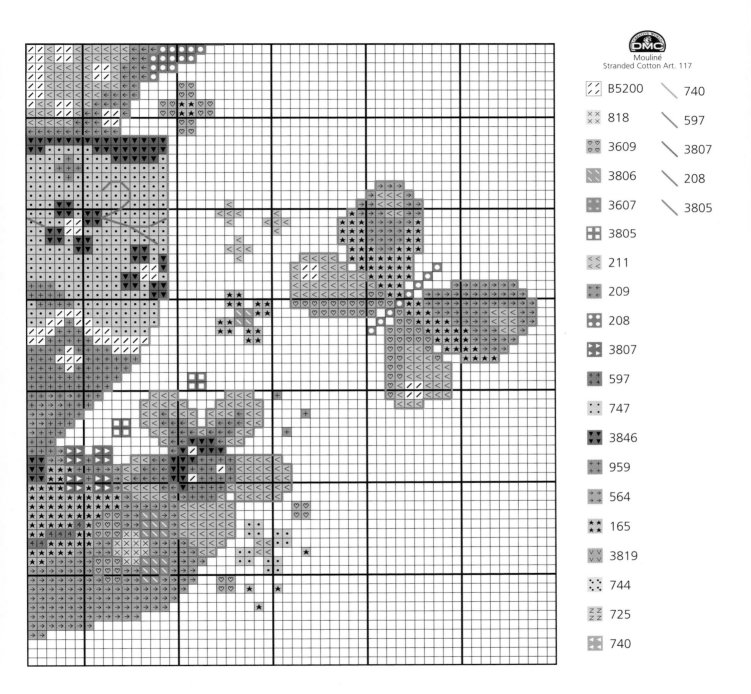

DMC
Mouliné
Stranded Cotton Art. 117

Symbol	Color	Symbol	Color
B5200	\ 740
818	\ 597
3609	\ 3807
3806	\ 208
3607	\ 3805
3805	
211	
209	
208	
3807	
597	
747	
3846	
959	
564	
165	
3819	
744	
725	
740	

48

Floral Sewing Machine

My sewing machine sits by the window in the studio overlooking the garden. This is where I took my inspiration for this design. I love to fill my home with pots of freshly cut blooms and watch the butterflies dance around the flower beds outside while I work.

There are lots of interesting elements within this design that could be used on other things. The pin cushion could be stitched separately and added to the front of a needle case and a single butterfly would make a lovely greeting card.

Fabric DMC 28 ct Linen DM432/B5200
Fabric Size 42 x 48 cm
Pattern Size 19,5 x 26 cm
Thread DMC Stranded Cotton

Cross Stitch 2 strands
Backstitch 1 strand

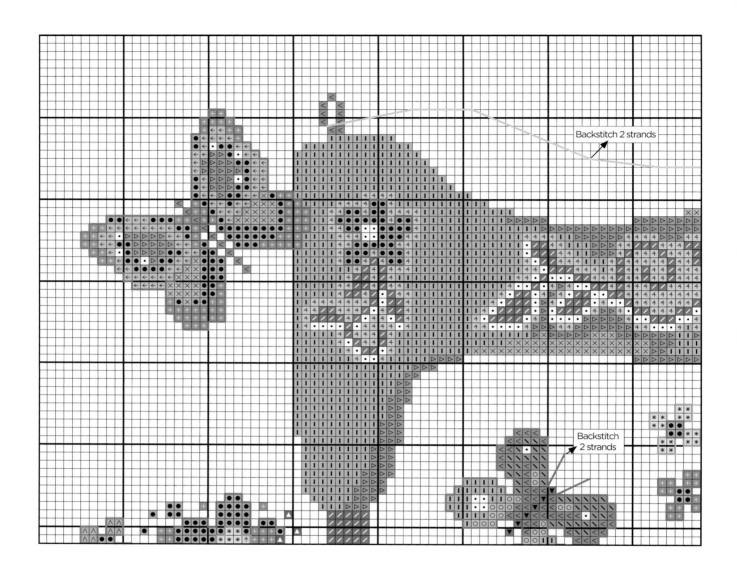

Backstitch 2 strands

Backstitch
2 strands

⠒⠒ B5200	×× 955	▼▼ 3846	3807	←← 3689	740	╱ 3807
** 727	◀◀ 913	▮▮ 3761	∘∘ 211	>> 819	╱ 211	╱ 3805
↑↑ 726	╱╱ 3849	4 4 747	╲╲ 209	3806	╱ 3849	╱ 740
⋀⋀ 3819	▷▷ 959	<< 340	•• 3609	▲ 3805	╱ 906	

DMC
Mouliné
Stranded Cotton Art. 117

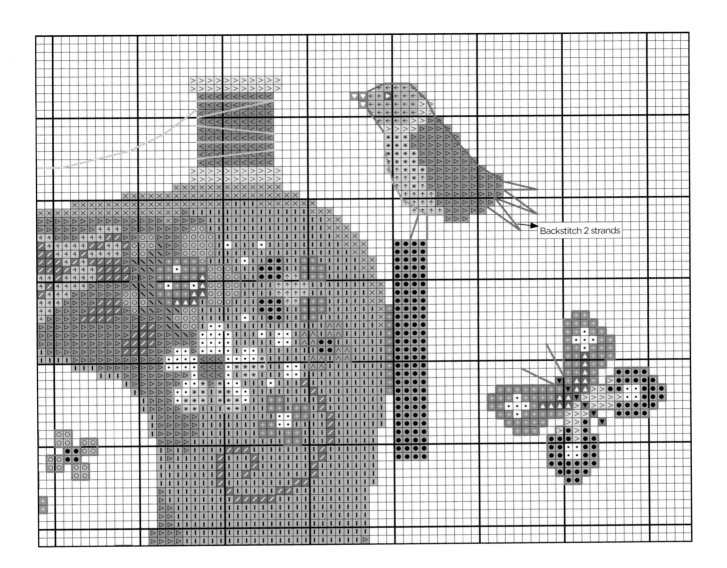

Backstitch 2 strands

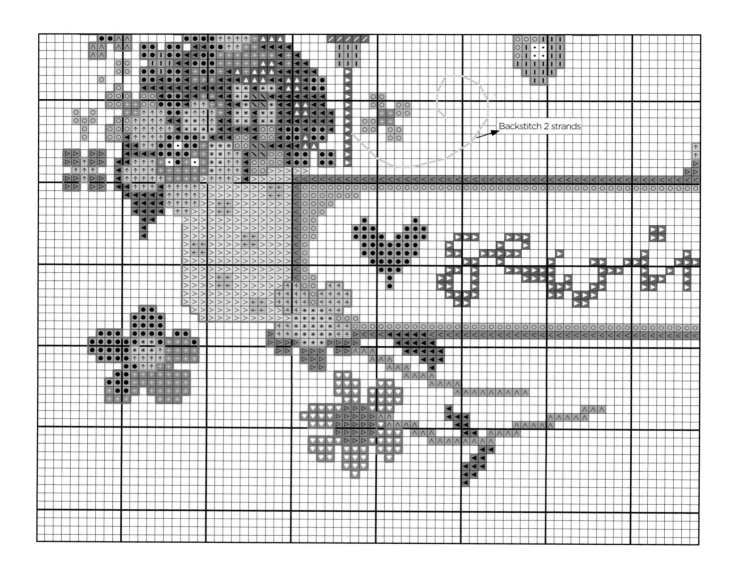

Backstitch 2 strands

:: B5200	×× 955	▼▼ 3846	3807	3689	740	╱ 3807
** 727	◄◄ 913	┃┃ 3761	←← 211	>> 819	╱ 211	╱ 3805
↑↑ 726	╱╱ 3849	4 4 747	╲╲ 209	++ 3806	╱ 3849	╱ 740
∧∧ 3819	▷▷ 959	≪≪ 340	•• 3609	▲▲ 3805	╱ 906	

DMC
Mouliné
Stranded Cotton Art. 117

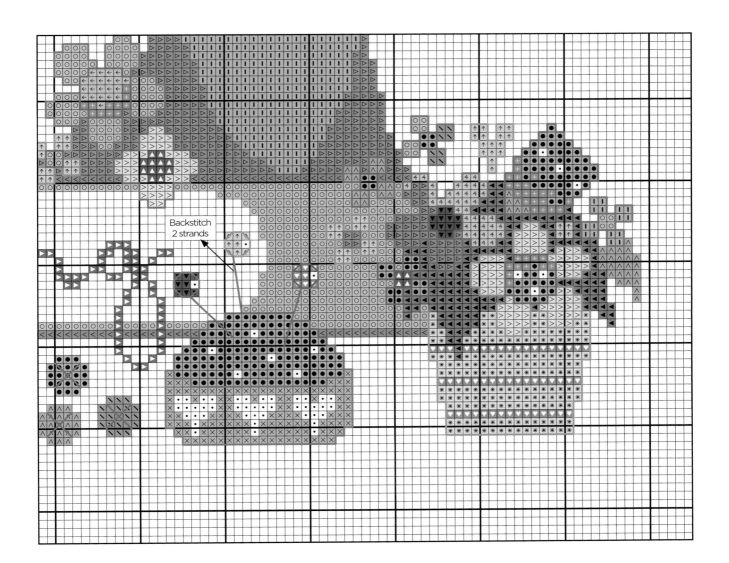

Backstitch
2 strands

Afternoon Tea

With it's pretty china teapot and scrummy cup cakes, this design reflects the joy of afternoon tea. The lovely pastel colours and the striped and spotted bunting give the design a light summery feel. Some of the details, such as the butterfly and the cup cake, could be stitched individually and used as an embellishment for a greeting card

Fabric DMC 28 ct Linen DM432/B5200
Fabric Size 40 x 40 cm
Pattern Size 17,5 x 19 cm
Thread DMC Stranded Cotton

Cross Stitch 2 strands
Backstitch 1 strand

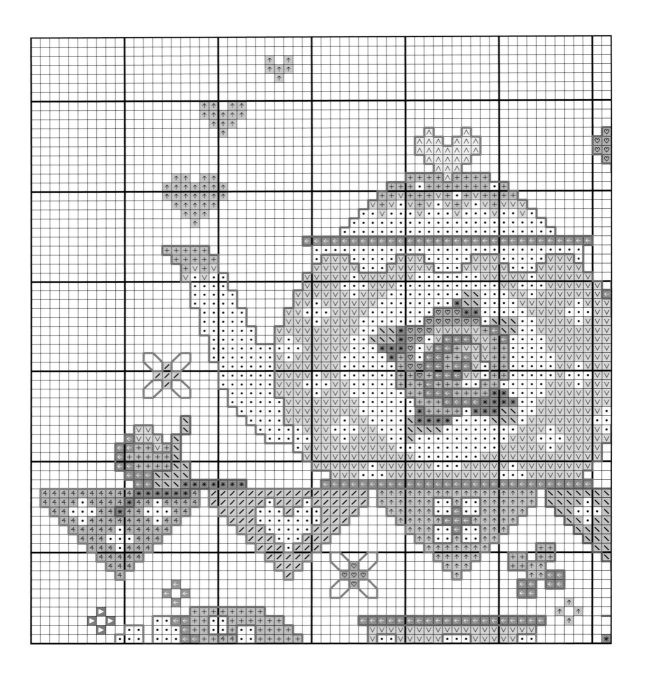

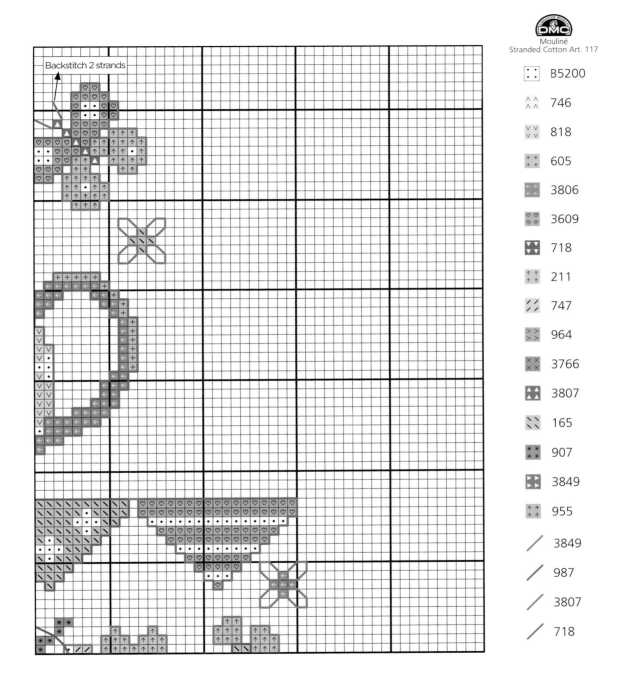

DMC
Mouliné
Stranded Cotton Art. 117

Backstitch 2 strands

∷	B5200
^ ^	746
v v	818
+ +	605
← ←	3806
♡ ♡	3609
▼ ▼	718
↑ ↑	211
╱ ╱	747
> >	964
✕ ✕	3766
▲ ▲	3807
╲ ╲	165
✳ ✳	907
❖	3849
⁴ ⁴	955
╱	3849
╱	987
╱	3807
╱	718

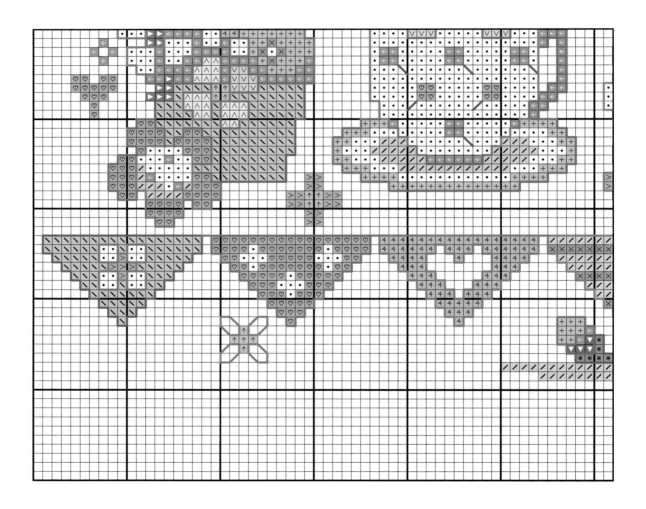

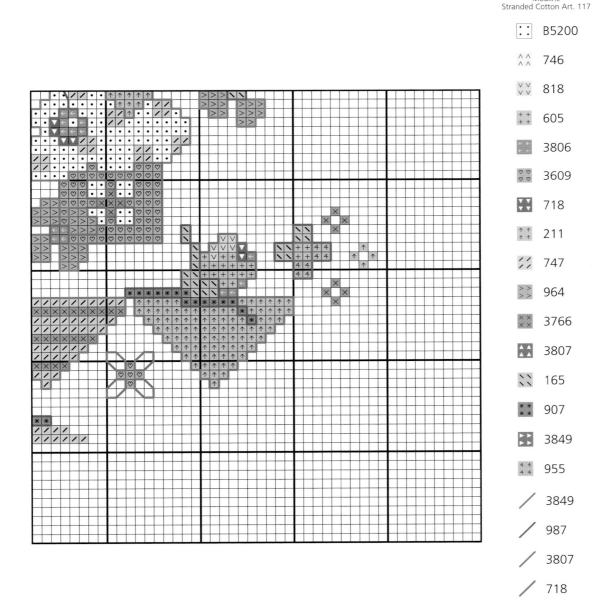

DMC
Mouliné
Stranded Cotton Art. 117

::	B5200
^^	746
vv	818
++	605
←	3806
♡♡	3609
▼▼	718
↑↑	211
⁄⁄	747
>>	964
✕✕	3766
▲▲	3807
＼＼	165
✱✱	907
✾✾	3849
44	955
╱	3849
╱	987
╱	3807
╱	718

Baby Boy
Teddy Bear Sampler

Who can resist teddy bears ! These cute bears are here to celebrate the baby's birth. They are decked in bright blue romper suits and have a shiny blue toy car each.

This sampler can be easily personalised by using the alphabet provided and the weight of the baby and date of birth can be added.

Real buttons could be added in place of the stitched versions at the corners of the floor mat and felt hearts could replace the hearts hanging from the tree to add interest to your finished piece.

Fabric DMC 16 ct Aida DM844/Blanc
Fabric Size 42 x 42 cm
Pattern Size 19,5 x 20 cm
Thread DMC Stranded Cotton

Cross Stitch 2 strands
Backstitch 1 strand

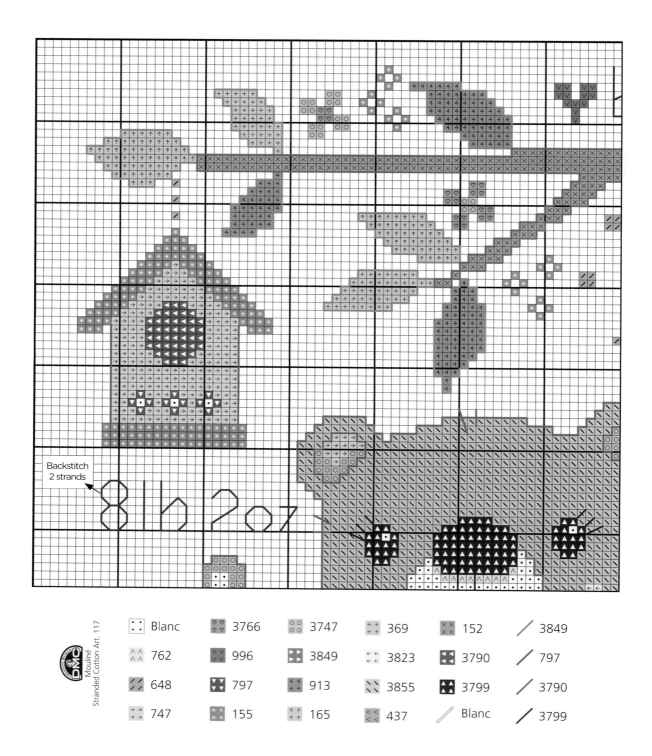

Backstitch
2 strands

8lb 2oz

DMC
Mouliné
Stranded Cotton Art. 117

Symbol	Color	Symbol	Color	Symbol	Color	Symbol	Color	Symbol	Color	Symbol	Color
::	Blanc	♥♥	3766	○○	3747	++	369	××	152	/	3849
^^	762	∨∨	996	✳	3849	⇇	3823	▨	3790	/	797
⁄⁄	648	▼	797	44	913	＼＼	3855	▲▲	3799	/	3790
→→	747	✳	155	↑↑	165	<<	437	⫽	Blanc	/	3799

62

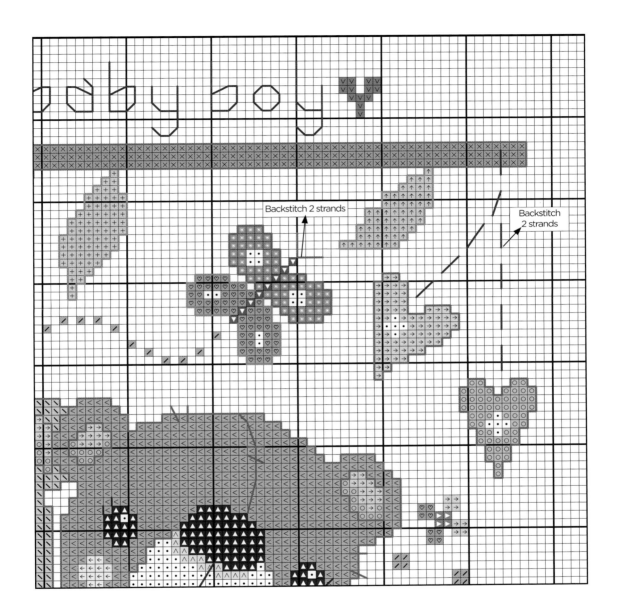

Backstitch 2 strands

Backstitch
2 strands

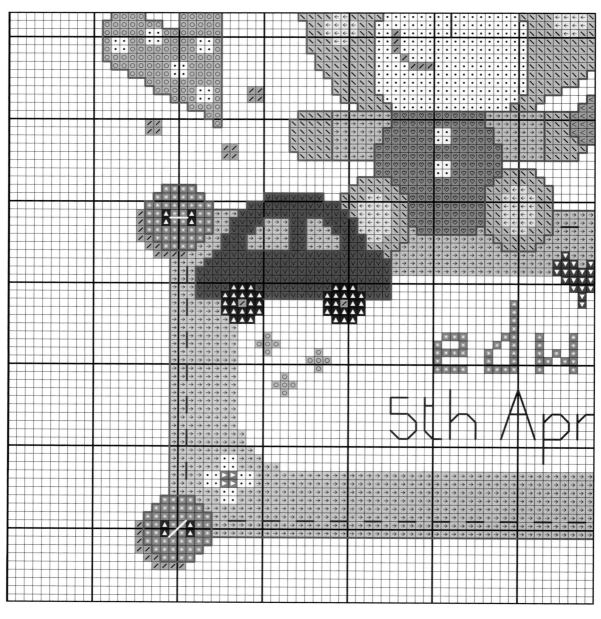

Mouliné
Stranded Cotton Art. 117

∴ Blanc	♥ 3766	◦◦ 3747	++ 369	✕✕ 152	╱ 3849
∧∧ 762	∨∨ 996	3849	← 3823	3790	╱ 797
╱╱ 648	797	++ 913	↘↘ 3855	▲▲ 3799	╱ 3790
→ 747	✳ 155	↑↑ 165	≪ 437	╱ Blanc	╱ 3799

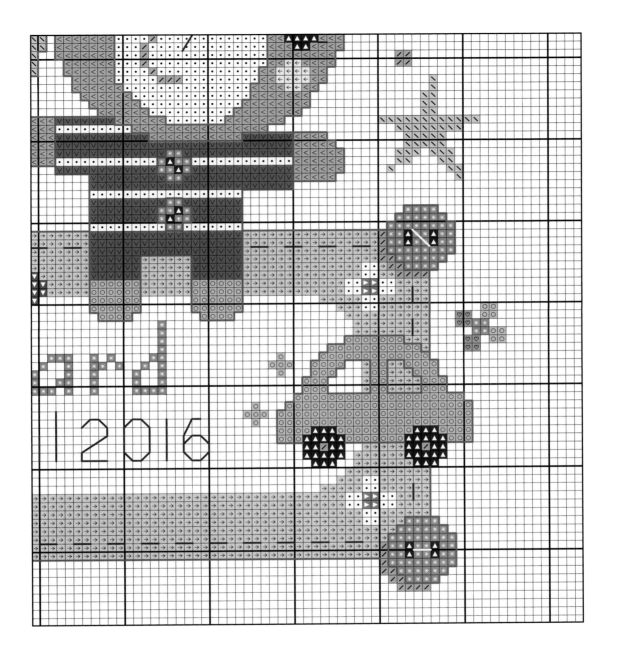

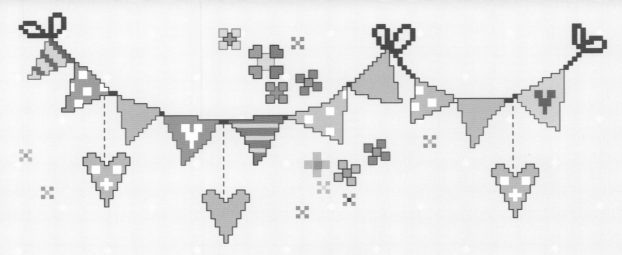

Floral Bicycle

This design came from my love of the outdoors. In the summer I like to get my bicycle out and cycle down the promenade next to the sea where I live.

The bunting and the flowers give the whole piece a lovely summery feel and this design is full of interesting elements to stitch. This piece would look great framed and hung on a sunny wall or alternatively it could be bordered with soft fabric and made into a cushion. The bunting could be replaced with appliquéd scraps of spotted and striped fabric to add extra interest.

Fabric DMC 16 ct Aida DM844/Blanc
Fabric Size 42 x 45 cm
Pattern Size 19,5 x 21,5 cm
Thread DMC Stranded Cotton

Cross Stitch 2 strands
Backstitch 1 strand

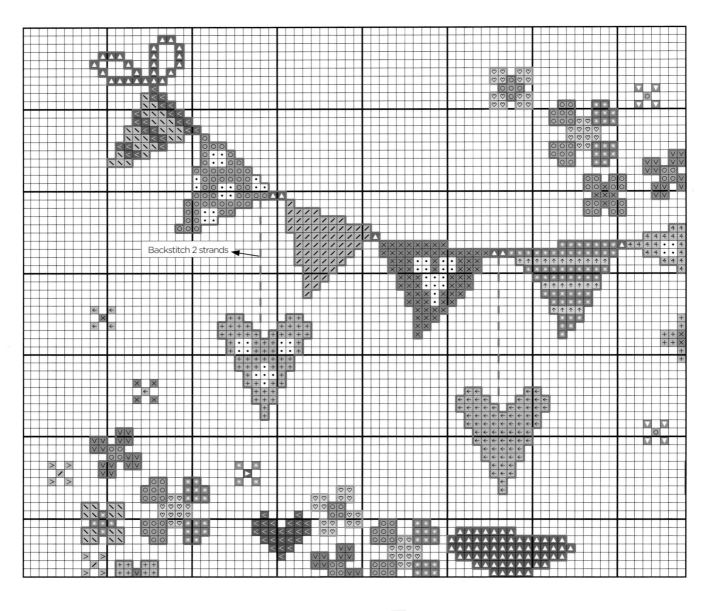

Backstitch 2 strands

$\because$ B5200	3849	744	605	211	718
^^ 762	166	740	3609	3807	3849
747	165	3824	3806	988	3807
3766	369	818	718	740	

DMC
Mouliné
Stranded Cotton Art. 117

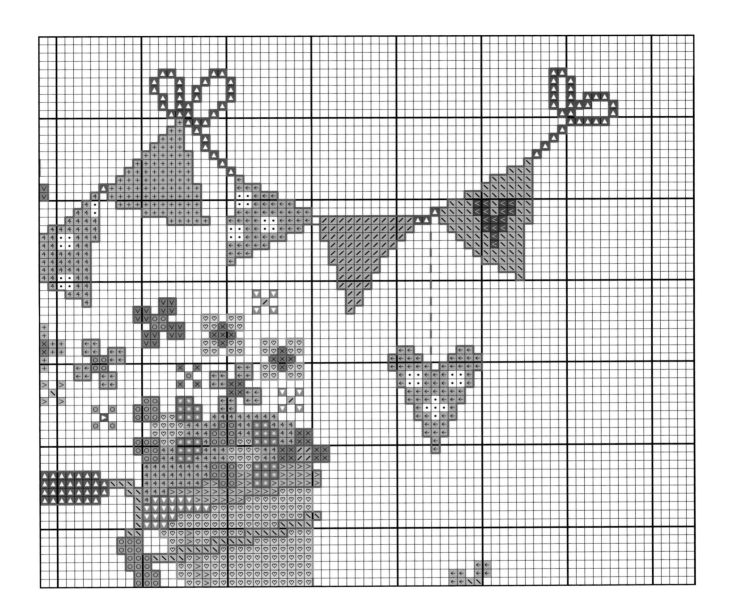

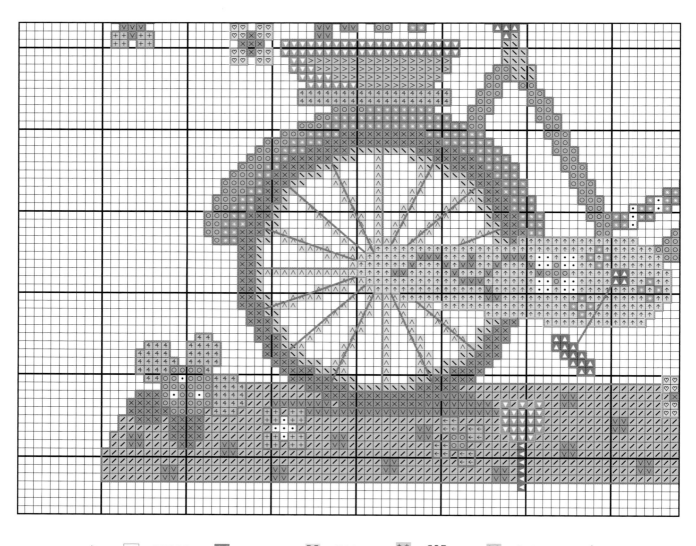

Symbol	Code	Symbol	Code	Symbol	Code	Symbol	Code	Symbol	Code	Symbol	Code
:	B5200	✕	3849	♡	744	+	605	←	211	/	718
^	762	∨	166	▼	740	⊙	3609	▲	3807	/	3849
\	747	/	165	>	3824	▦	3806	/	988	/	3807
✕	3766	↟	369	↑	818	◆	718	/	740		

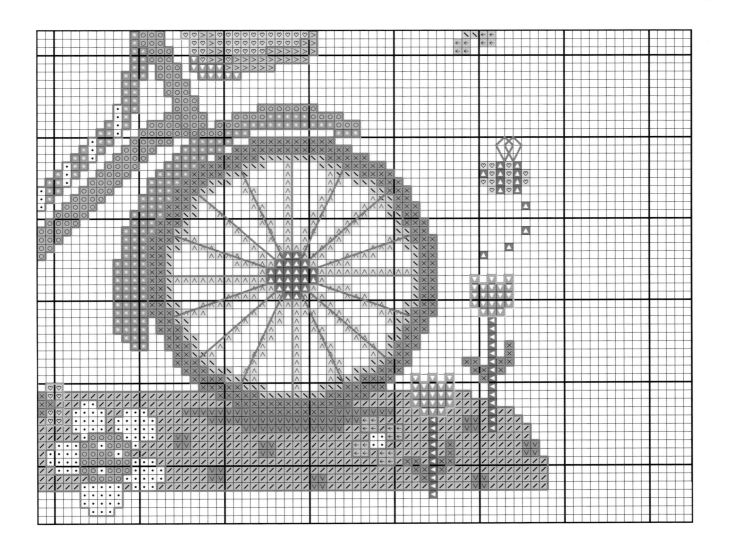

Baby Girl
Teddy Bear Sampler

These two cute and cuddly teddies are here to celebrate the baby's birth. Pretty in pink and surrounded by butterflies and flowers, they would make a lovely addition to any little girl's nursery.

This sampler can be easily personalised by using the alphabet provided and the weight of the baby and date of birth can be added. Real buttons could be added in place of the stitched versions at the corners of the floor mat and felt hearts could replace the hearts hanging from the tree to add interest to your finished piece.

Fabric DMC 16 ct Aida DM844/Blanc
Fabric Size 42 x 42 cm
Pattern Size 19,5 x 20 cm
Thread DMC Stranded Cotton

Cross Stitch 2 strands
Backstitch 1 strand

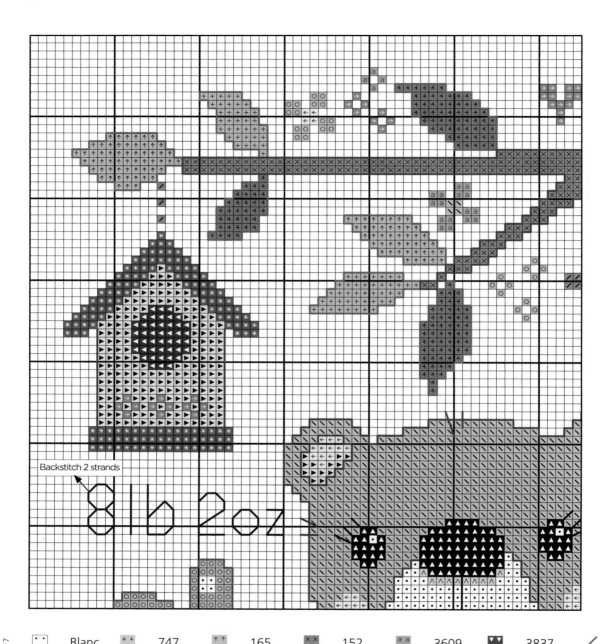

Backstitch 2 strands

8lb 2oz

DMC
Mouliné
Stranded Cotton Art. 117

Blanc	747	165	152	3609	3837	3805
762	964	3823	3790	3806	Blanc	3799
648	913	3855	819	3805	3849	3837
3799	369	437	3689	211	3790	

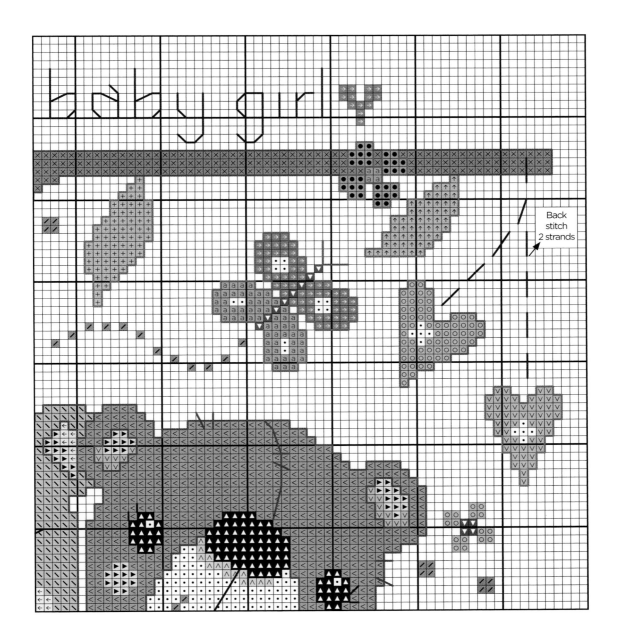

Back
stitch
2 strands

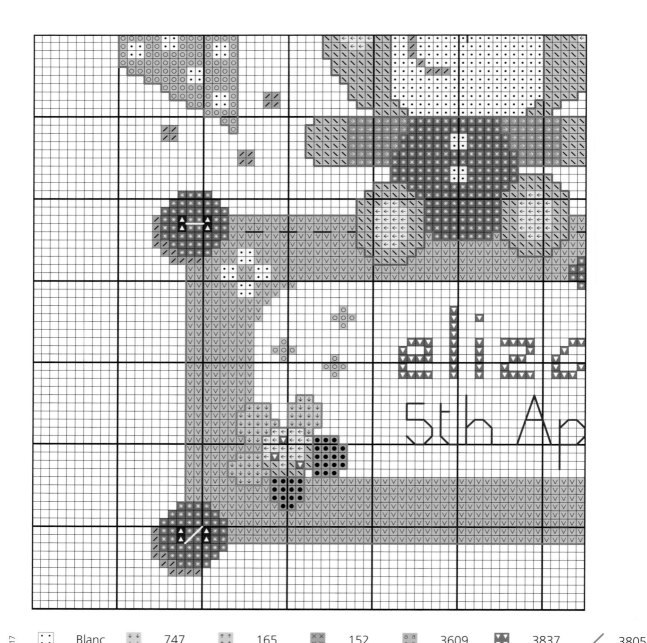

Mouliné
Stranded Cotton Art. 117

::	Blanc	↓↓	747	↑↑	165	××	152	aa	3609	▨	3837	╱	3805
∧∧	762	●●	964	←←	3823	❋	3790	→→	3806	╱	Blanc	╱	3799
∥∥	648	44	913	◣◣	3855	▶▶	819	**	3805	╱	3849	╱	3837
▨	3799	++	369	<<	437	vv	3689	○○	211	╱	3790		

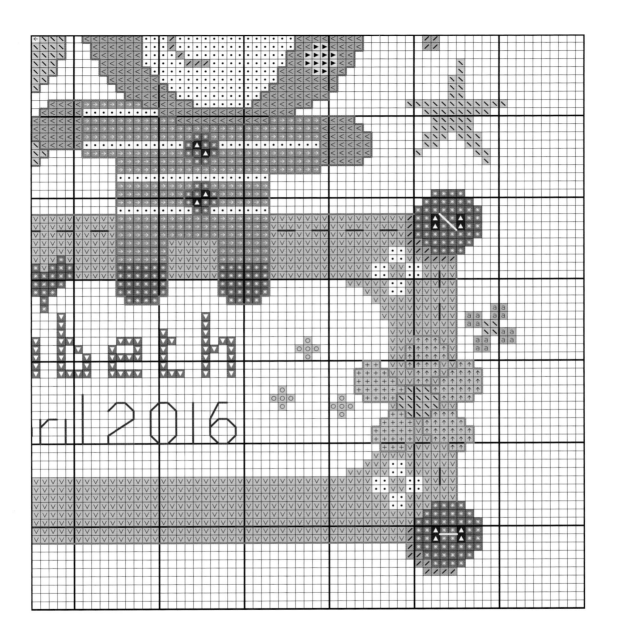

sweet
dreams

25th
feb
2016

7lb
4oz

alfie

Baby Boy Sweet Dreams

This charming baby boy sampler would make a lovely addition to any nursery. Alongside the cute little train and the small blue cars, the stitched quilt also contains panels where you can add the baby's birth date and weight. You can also easily add the baby's name by using the alphabet chart provided.

Real buttons could be added to the sampler in place of the stitched ones to give the finished piece a more handmade feel.

Fabric DMC 16 ct Aida DM844/Blanc
Fabric Size 35 x 50 cm
Pattern Size 13,5 x 28 cm
Thread DMC Stranded Cotton

Cross Stitch 2 strands
Backstitch 1 strand

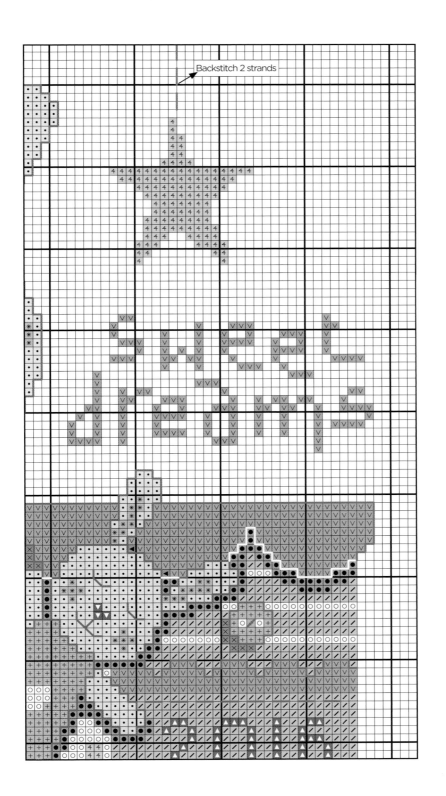

DMC
Mouliné
Stranded Cotton Art. 117

○○	B5200
∴	712
✳✳	754
♥♥	611
●●	164
\\	165
∕∕	772
◀◀	959
∨∨	964
♡♡	747
<<	162
++	3747
✕✕	340
▲▲	333
4 4	726
╱	B5200
╱	581
╱	3812
╱	333
╱	611

Backstitch 2 strands

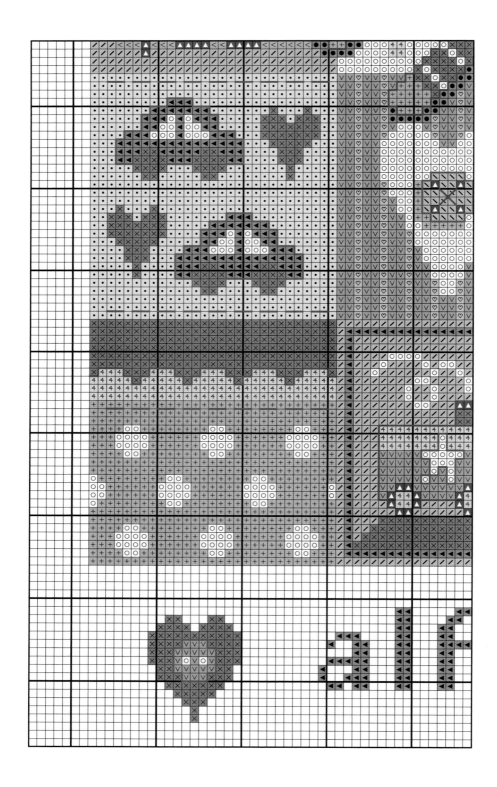

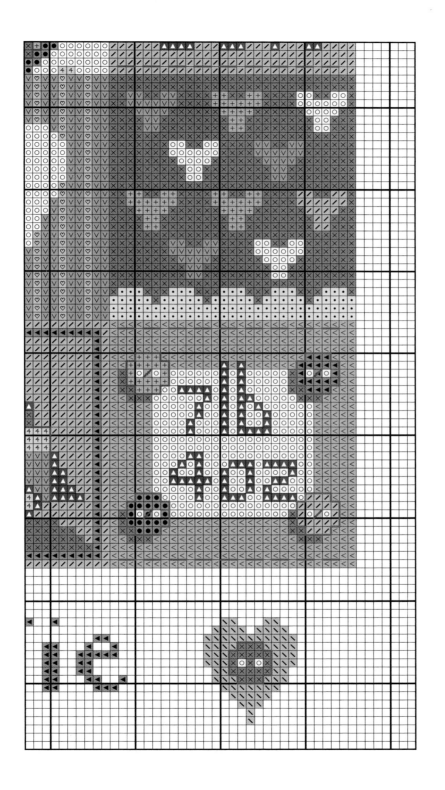

Mouliné
Stranded Cotton Art. 117

B5200
712
754
611
164
165
772
959
964
747
162
3747
340
333
726
B5200
581
3812
333
611

Baby Girl Sweet Dreams

This adorable baby girl sampler would make a lovely addition to any nursery. Delicate hearts and flowers and a pretty pink butterfly adorn the quilt where the baby rabbit sleeps. There are also spaces added within the quilt where you can add the baby's birth date and weight.

The design can also be easily personalised by using the alphabet provided. Heart shaped buttons could be used to replace some of the stitched ones within the quilt to give a more 3d hand crafted feel, and a felt flower could be added in the bottom panel instead of a stitched one.

Fabric DMC 16 ct Aida DM844/Blanc
Fabric Size 35 x 50 cm
Pattern Size 13,5 x 28 cm
Thread DMC Stranded Cotton

Cross Stitch 2 strands
Backstitch 1 strand

Backstitch 2 strands

Mouliné
Stranded Cotton Art. 117

○○ ○○	B5200
:: ::	712
** **	754
∥ ∥	3689
++ ++	605
4 4	3806
∧∧ ∧∧	3609
∖∖ ∖∖	211
×× ××	209
▼▼ ▼▼	3837
▲▲ ▲▲	611
∨∨ ∨∨	727
/	B5200
/	3837
/	611
/	601

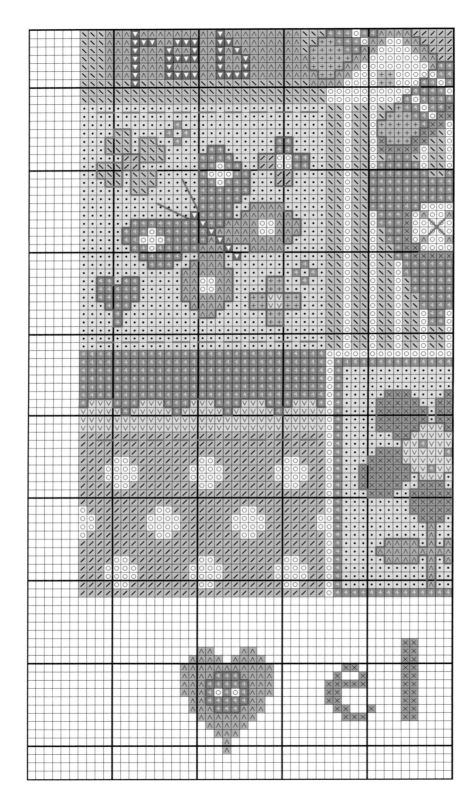

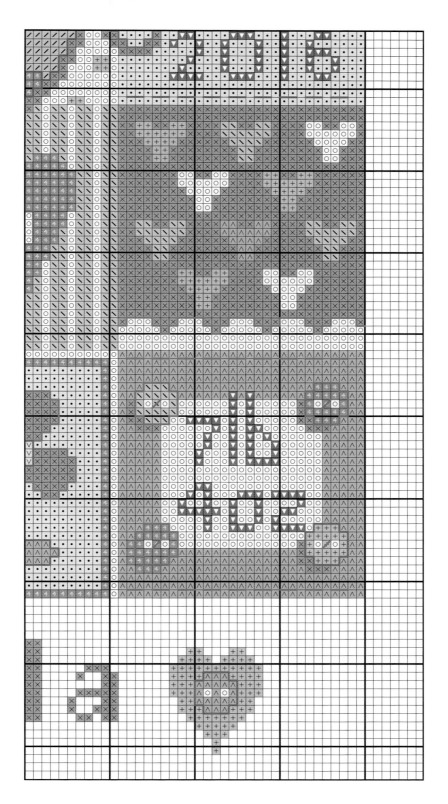

Mouliné
Stranded Cotton Art. 117

○ ○	B5200
: :	712
＊＊	754
∕∕	3689
+ +	605
4 4	3806
∧ ∧	3609
＼＼	211
✕✕	209
▼▼	3837
▲▲	611
∨∨	727
∕	B5200
∕	3837
∕	611
∕	601

Love

This celebration of love includes lots of interesting elements to stitch such as the tiny hearts, pretty daises and buttercups. The pretty pastel colours are influenced by the flowers within my own garden. This design would make a perfect wedding gift and could be easily personalised by using one of the alphabets contained within this book.

Alternatively you could add it to the front of a photo album as a keepsake or make into a cushion and display it within your home.

Fabric DMC 16 ct Aida DM844/Blanc
Fabric Size 35 x 50 cm
Pattern Size 14 x 28 cm
Thread DMC Stranded Cotton

Cross Stitch 2 strands
Backstitch 1 strand

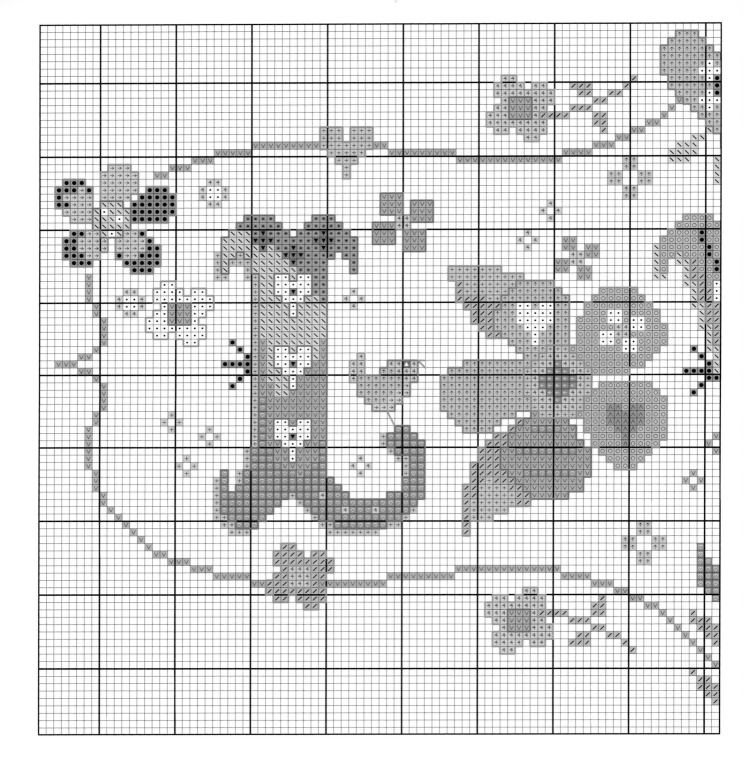

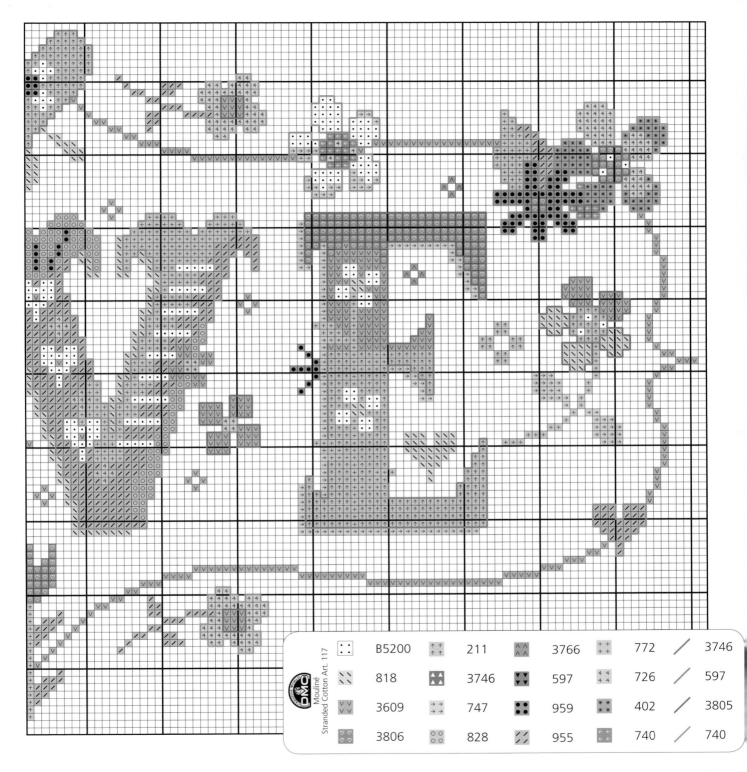

Floral Dress

This pretty summer dress design is a joy to stitch. It is evocative of summer days, with its sweet full blooms and delicate butterflies. The pretty pink tones used within its stitches make this a very soft and feminine design.

It would make a lovely gift for a birthday or wedding. The single shoe could be stitched on its own and used on a gift tag or greeting card.

Fabric DMC 16 ct Aida DM844/Blanc
Fabric Size 40 x 45 cm
Pattern Size 18 x 23,5 cm
Thread DMC Stranded Cotton

Cross Stitch 2 strands
Backstitch 1 strand

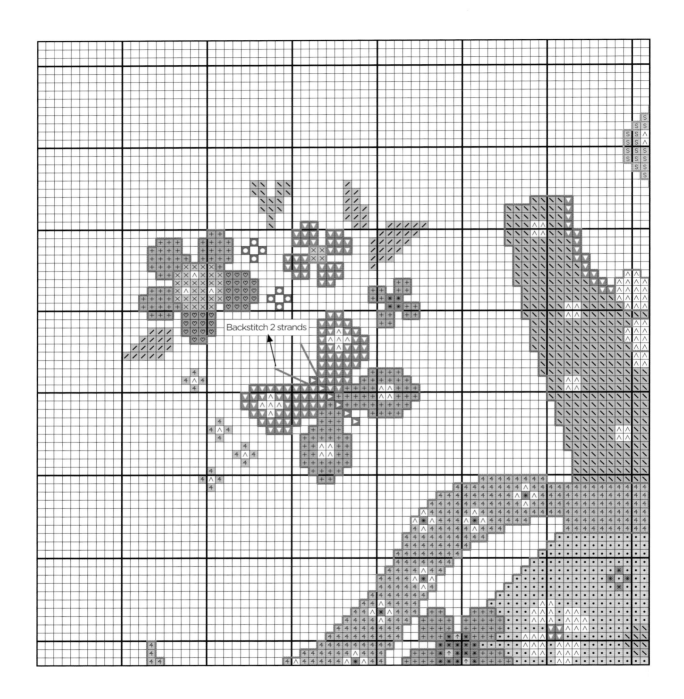

Backstitch 2 strands

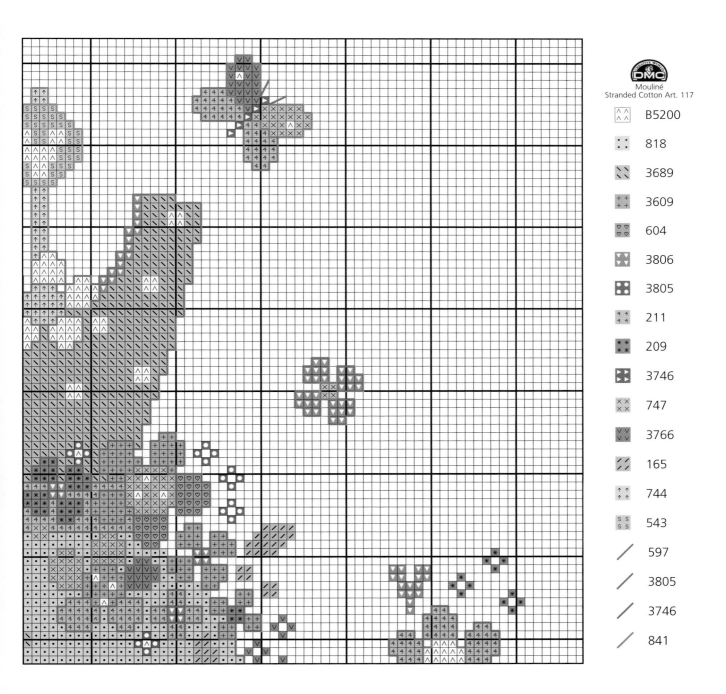

DMC
Mouliné
Stranded Cotton Art. 117

Symbol	Code
^ ^	B5200
::	818
\ \	3689
+ +	3609
♥ ♥	604
▼▼	3806
::	3805
4 4	211
* *	209
►◄	3746
× ×	747
v v	3766
⁄⁄	165
↑ ↑	744
s s	543
⁄	597
⁄	3805
⁄	3746
⁄	841

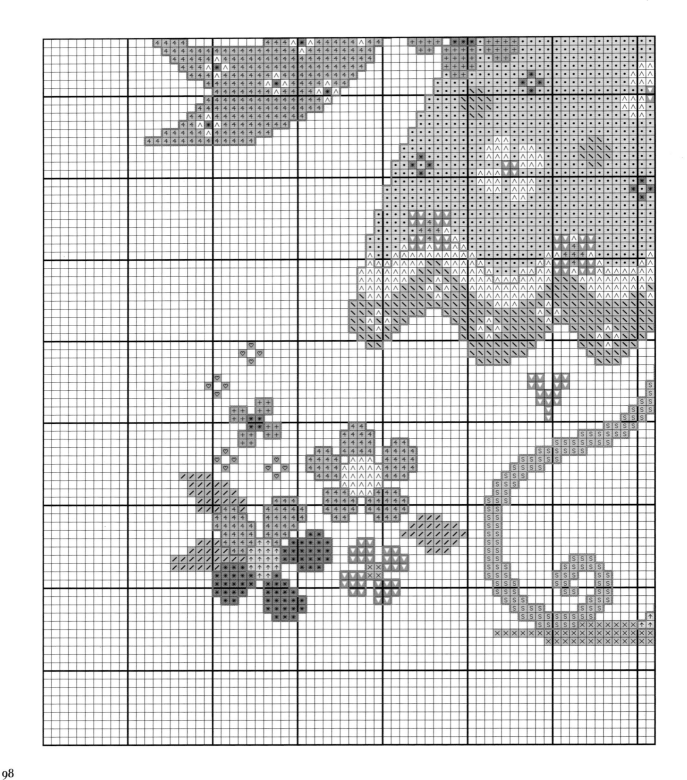

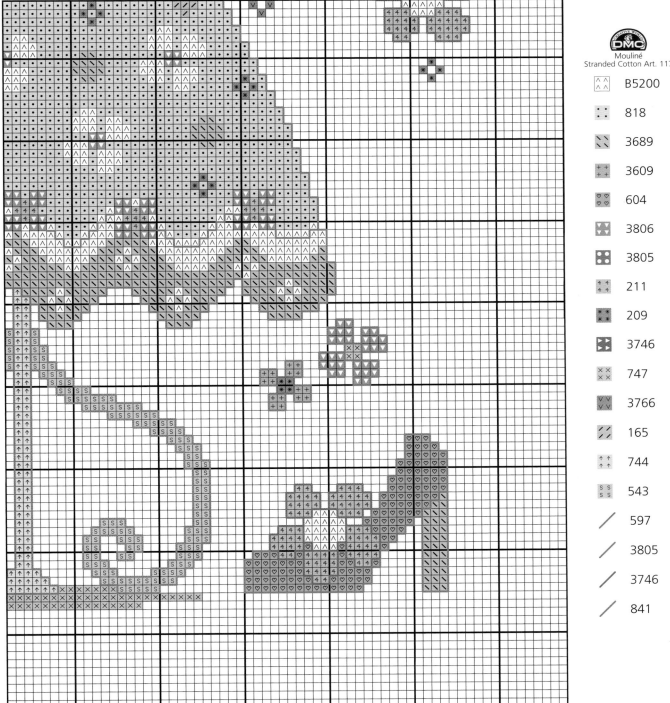

DMC
Mouliné
Stranded Cotton Art. 117

Symbol	Color
^ ^	B5200
: :	818
\ \	3689
+ +	3609
♥ ♥	604
▼ ▼	3806
⊠ ⊠	3805
4 4	211
✳ ✳	209
◨ ◨	3746
✕ ✕	747
V V	3766
⁄ ⁄	165
↑ ↑	744
S S	543
⁄	597
⁄	3805
⁄	3746
⁄	841

Summer Love

This design is my version of the traditional floral wreath. One of my favourite flowers from the garden is the hydrangea so I have included them within this mass of blooms.

The tiny delicate butterflies dotted through this design could be stitched separately and added to gift tags or greeting cards. This design would make an ideal keepsake if stitched for a wedding.

The names and date could be easily added in the centre using one of the alphabets provided within this book.

Fabric DMC 16 ct Aida DM844/Blanc
Fabric Size 42 x 42 cm
Pattern Size 21 x 24 cm
Thread DMC Stranded Cotton

Cross Stitch 2 strands
Backstitch 1 strand

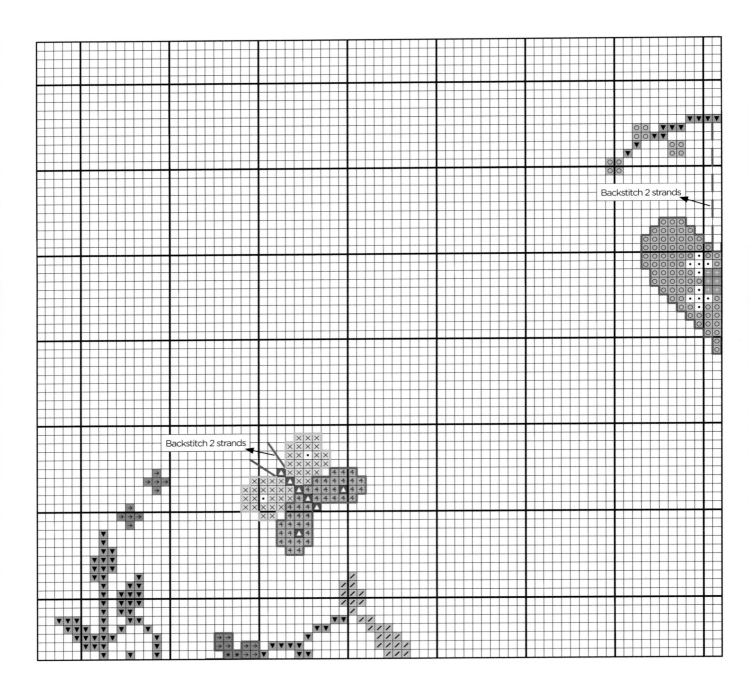

Backstitch 2 strands

Backstitch 2 strands

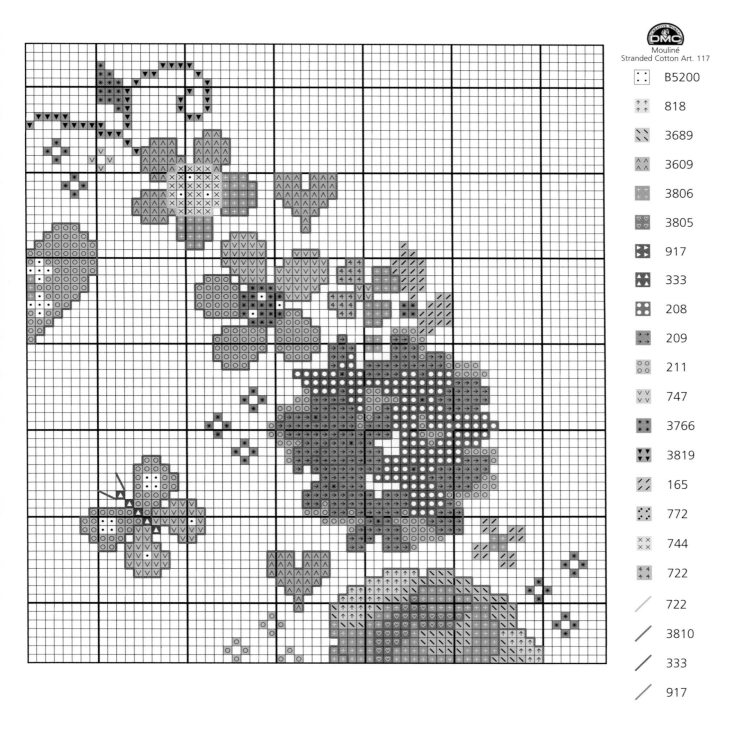

Mouliné
Stranded Cotton Art. 117

::	B5200
↑↑	818
＼＼	3689
∧∧	3609
++	3806
♡♡	3805
✦✦	917
▲▲	333
⊞⊞	208
→→	209
∘∘	211
∨∨	747
✴✴	3766
▼▼	3819
∕∕	165
∴∴	772
✕✕	744
44	722
╱	722
╱	3810
╱	333
╱	917

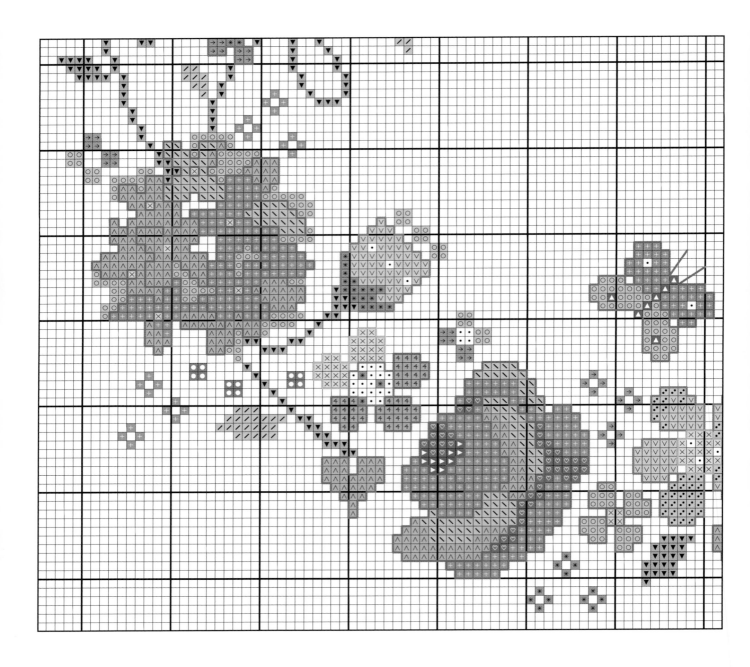

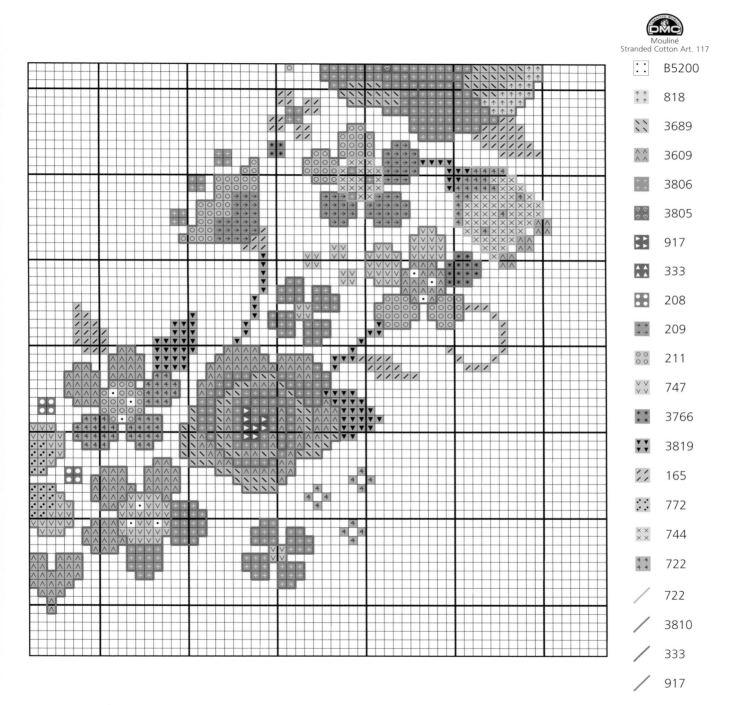

Mouliné
Stranded Cotton Art. 117

Symbol	Color
⠒	B5200
↑↑	818
＼＼	3689
∧∧	3609
＋＋	3806
♡♡	3805
✦	917
▲▲	333
⊞	208
→→	209
○○	211
∨∨	747
＊＊	3766
▼▼	3819
／／	165
⠿	772
××	744
44	722
／	722
／	3810
／	333
／	917

Cup Cake Sampler

This design is inspired by my passion for baking. The cakes are festooned with brightly coloured icing, jelly hearts and fresh fruit and topped with sprinkles.

The pretty delicate flowers and pastel colours evoke the feeling of having tea and cake in a summer garden. The finished stitched design would make an ideal cover for a recipe journal or framed and hung in a baker's kitchen. Each cake could be stitched as a single design and used as a birthday card or on a gift tag.

Fabric DMC 16 ct Aida DM844/Blanc
Fabric Size 40 x 40 cm
Pattern Size 17 x 17 cm
Thread DMC Stranded Cotton

Cross Stitch 2 strands
Backstitch 1 strand

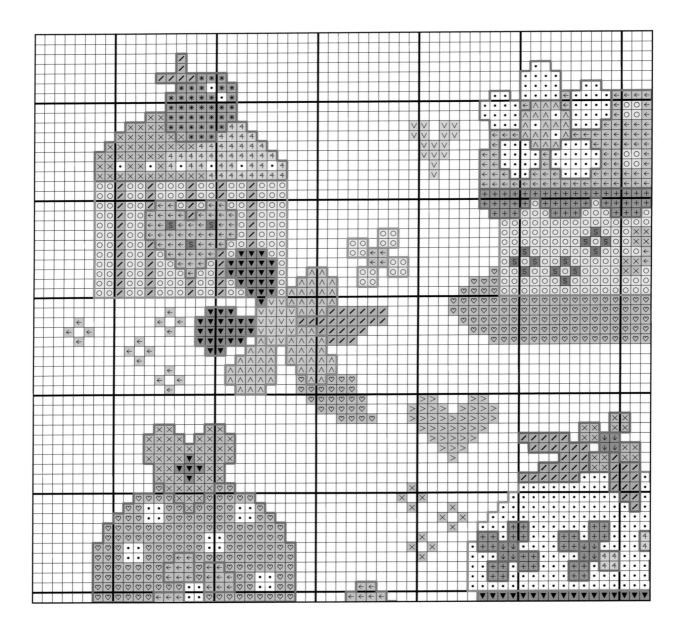

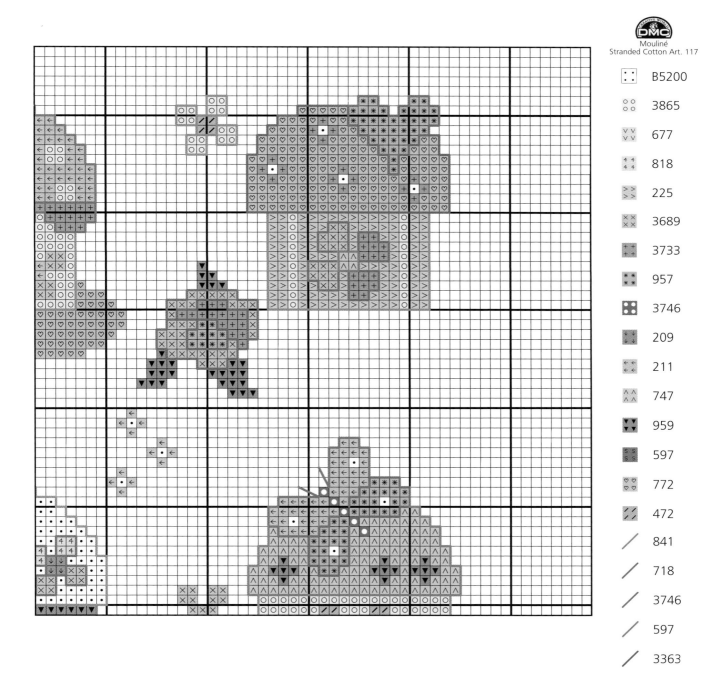

DMC
Mouliné
Stranded Cotton Art. 117

Symbol	Code
::	B5200
∘∘	3865
∨∨	677
＋＋	818
＞＞	225
××	3689
＋＋	3733
＊＊	957
⊞	3746
↓↓	209
↩↩	211
∧∧	747
▼▼	959
SS	597
♡♡	772
∕∕	472
∕	841
∕	718
∕	3746
∕	597
∕	3363

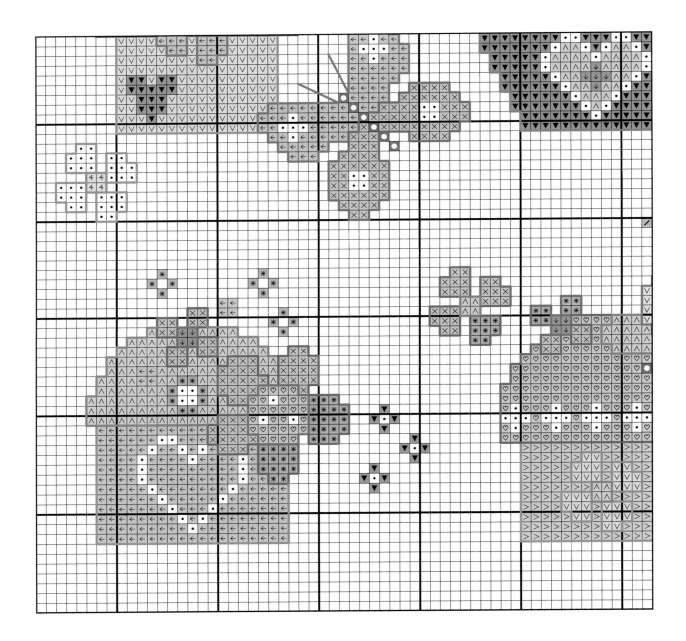

Mouliné
Stranded Cotton Art. 117

Symbol	Code
::	B5200
°°	3865
v v	677
4 4	818
> >	225
x x	3689
+ +	3733
* *	957
▦	3746
↓ ↓	209
← ←	211
∧ ∧	747
▼ ▼	959
s s	597
♡ ♡	772
⁄ ⁄	472
╱	841
╱	718
╱	3746
╱	597
╱	3363

Floral Wedding Sampler

This pretty floral design is a celebration of love. Ideal as a gift for a wedding, it can be personalised using the alphabet provided, and would look great framed or made into a cushion.

A single rose from this design could be stitched and made into a ring cushion to be used in the big day. The tiny butterfly could be stitched and added to a gift tag to compliment this stitched piece when giving as a gift.

Fabric DMC 16 ct Aida DM844/Blanc
Fabric Size 40 x 40 cm
Pattern Size 16,5 x 16,5 cm
Thread DMC Stranded Cotton

Cross Stitch 2 strands
Backstitch 1 strand

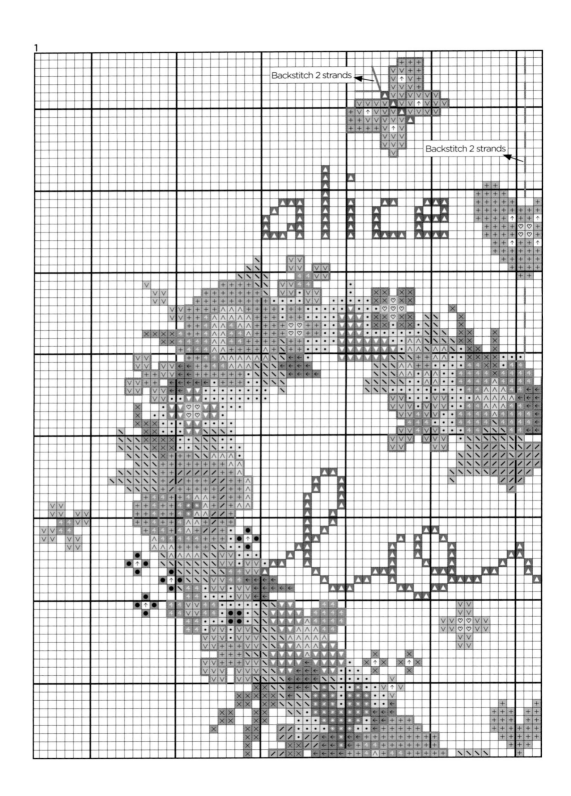

Backstitch 2 strands

Backstitch 2 strands

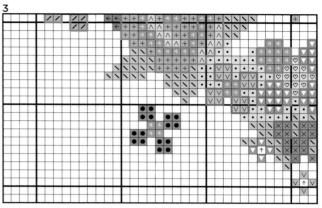
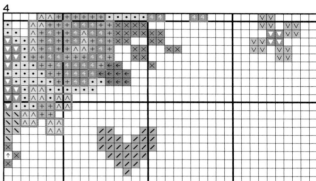

DMC
Mouliné
Stranded Cotton Art. 117

↑↑ / ↑↑	B5200	╱╱	772
∶∶	Ecru	← ←	913
∧∧ / ∧∧	818	●●	3766
╱╱	604	∨∨ / ∨∨	211
++ / ++	3609	✕✕	209
44 / 44	3806	▲▲	3837
✳✳ / ✳✳	3805	╱	970
▼▼ / ▼▼	956	╱	3805
♡♡ / ♡♡	744	╱	3837

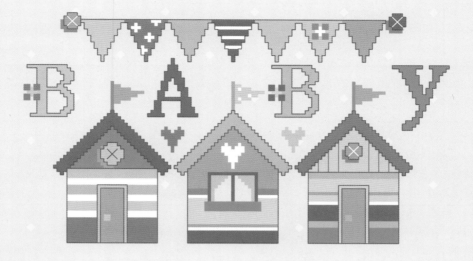

Baby Boy Seaside Sampler

This children's sampler was inspired by my early years living beside the sea. The combination of beach huts and bunting, alongside the subtle colour palette, give it a traditional nautical feel. Real buttons could be added instead of the stitched ones to give this design a more crafted 3d appearance.

The stitched piece can easily be personalised by adding the child's name using the alphabet chart provided and the hearts can be moved outwards to make way for a longer name. This design would look lovely as a framed piece or could be trimmed with soft blue fabric when finished and made into a cushion for the nursery.

Fabric DMC 16 ct Aida DM844/Blanc
Fabric Size 40 x 45 cm
Pattern Size 17 x 22 cm
Thread DMC Stranded Cotton

Cross Stitch 2 strands
Backstitch 1 strand

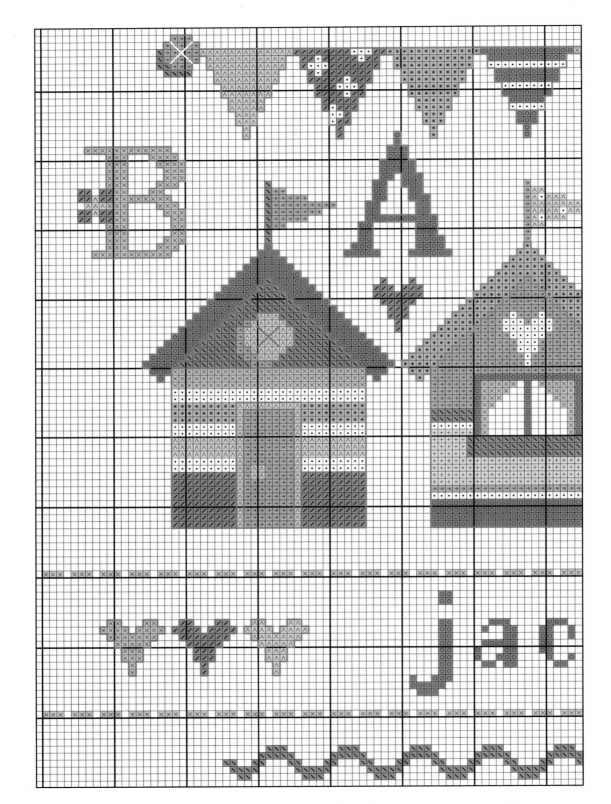

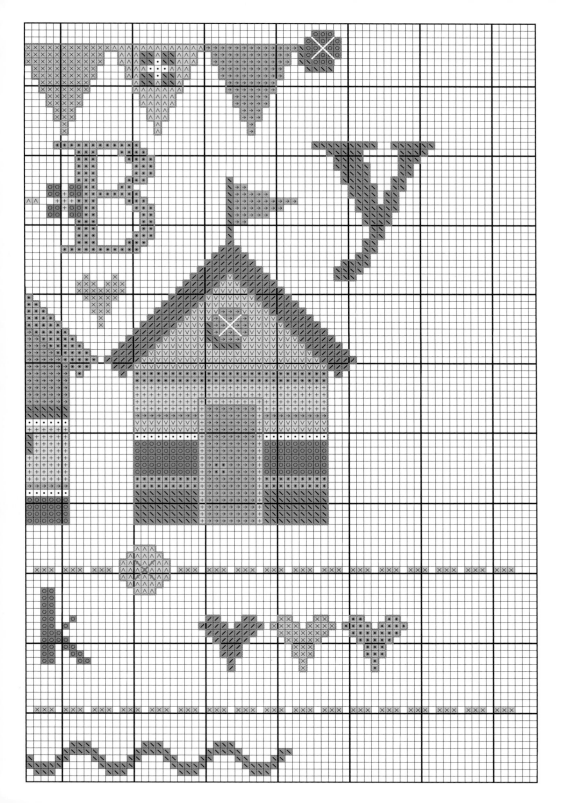

Mouliné
Stranded Cotton Art. 117

∴∴	B5200
∨∨ ∨∨	3756
×× ××	747
→→ →→	800
▨▨	3766
₀₀ ₀₀	809
◥◥	959
＊＊	772
∧∧ ∧∧	677
++ ++	Ecru
╱	B5200
╱	809
╱	647

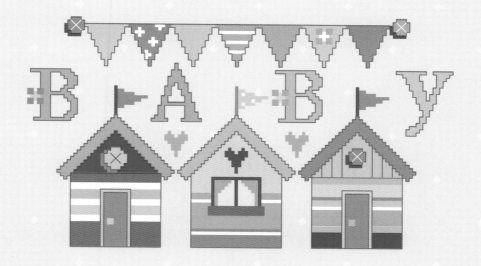

Baby Girl Seaside Sampler

The pink and pretty beach huts and stripy and spotted bunting make this adorable baby girl sampler a joy to stitch. It would look lovely framed on a nursery wall or stitched as a front piece for a baby journal as a keepsake. The stitched design can be easily personalised by using the alphabet provided and the hearts can be moved outwards to make way for a longer name.

Fabric DMC 16 ct Aida DM844/Blanc
Fabric Size 40 x 45 cm
Pattern Size 17 x 22 cm
Thread DMC Stranded Cotton

Cross Stitch 2 strands
Backstitch 1 strand

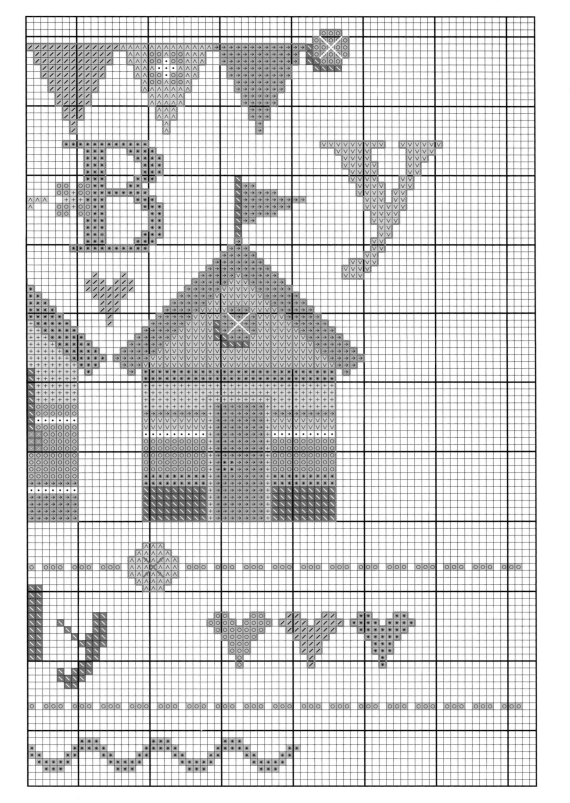

Mouliné
Stranded Cotton Art. 117

::	B5200
++	Ecru
∨∨	3713
○○	605
→→	3609
⤬⤬	3806
◥◥	602
⁄⁄	211
**	772
∧∧	677
⁄	B5200
⁄	602
⁄	647

Strawberry Tea

Strawberries are everyone's favourite. They are evocative of long summer days and garden parties on the lawn. This design includes many of the elements associated with that theme – cup cakes, strawberries and cream, delicate flowers and pretty butterflies.

There are lots of interesting elements to stitch within this piece and it would make an ideal addition to a kitchen when framed. You could replace the pink flowers within the border with felt flowers for extra interest.

Fabric DMC Aida DM222/Blanc
Fabric Size 35 x 40 cm
Pattern Size 11 x 16,5 cm
Thread DMC Stranded Cotton

Cross Stitch 2 strands
Backstitch 1 strand

DMC
Mouliné
Stranded Cotton Art. 117

Symbol	Code
::	B5200
^^	746
//	818
<<	605
44	3609
⟍⟍	3806
××	962
▼▼	3805
**	209
○○	211
♠♠	3746
∨∨	3766
↑↑	747
►►	3849
++	955
♡♡	165
●●	166
/	209
/	3849
/	987
/	3746
/	718
/	962

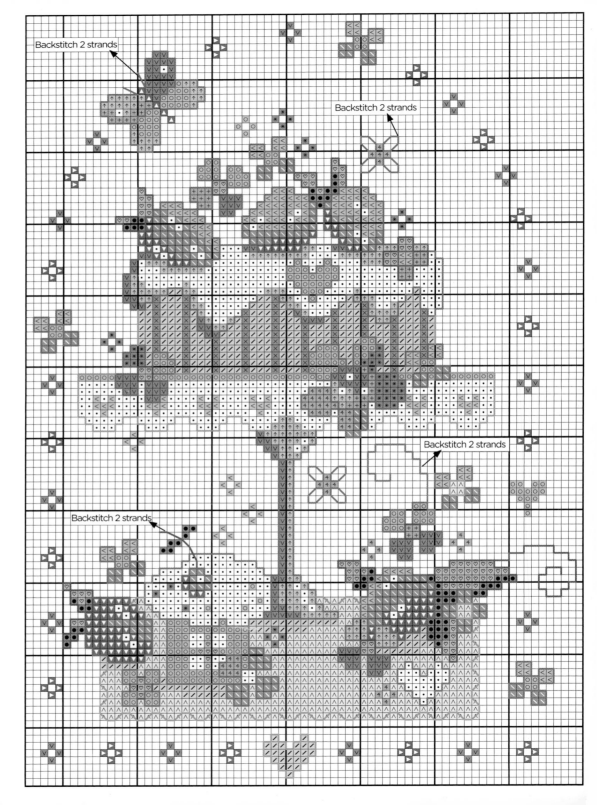

Alphabets

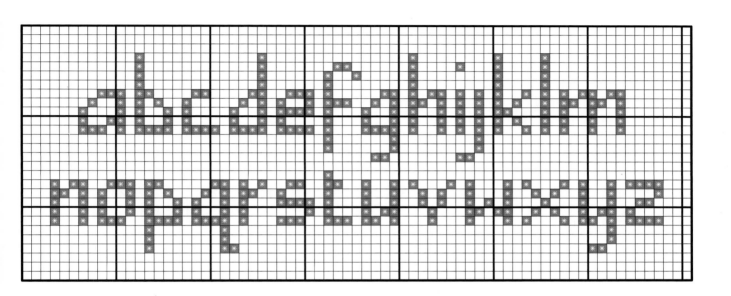

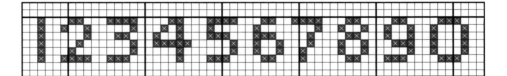

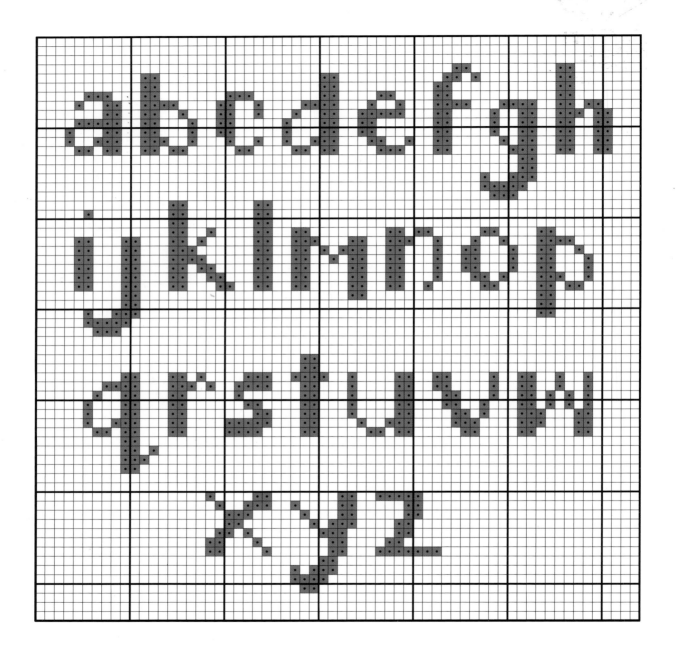